Dusk Aflame

poems & art

DUSK

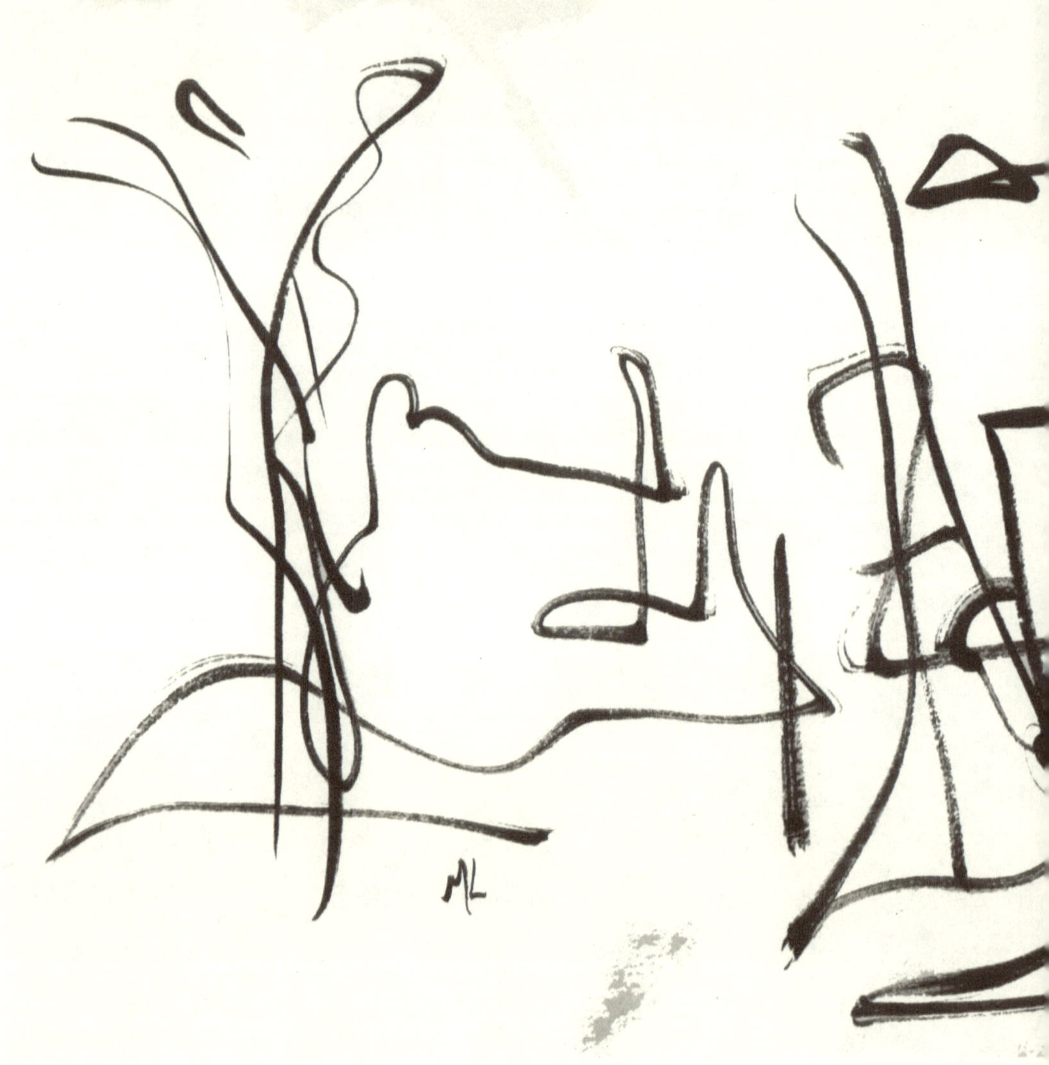

AFLAME

poems & art

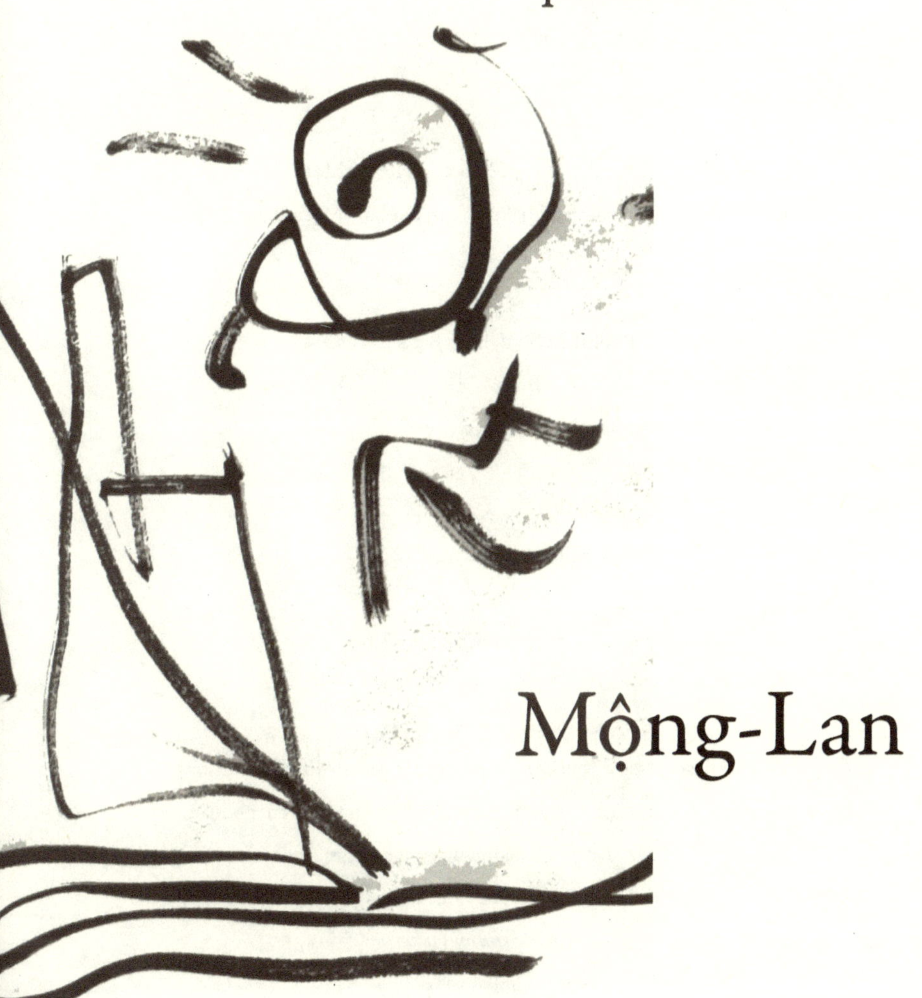

Mộng-Lan

Dusk Aflame: poems & art

Printed in the United States of America

ISBN-13: 978-0-9828227-4-6

Cover photo: "Buenos Aires at Dusk," 2017, by Mộng-Lan

Cover design, drawings and paintings in book by Mộng-Lan

Published by Valiant Press

PO Box 2771

Sugar Land, Texas 77487

Other Books by Mộng-Lan

Song of the Cicadas (Juniper Prize Winner)

Why is the Edge Always Windy?

Tango, Tangoing: Poems & Art

Tango, Tangueando: Poemas & Dibujos (bilingual Spanish-English edition)

Love Poem to Tofu & Other Poems (poetry & calligraphic art, chapbook)

Force of the Heart: Tango, Art (drawings, paintings, a poem)

Love Poem to Ginger & Other Poems (poetry & calligraphic art, chapbook)

One Thousand Minds Brimming: poems & art

www.monglan.com

for my loved ones

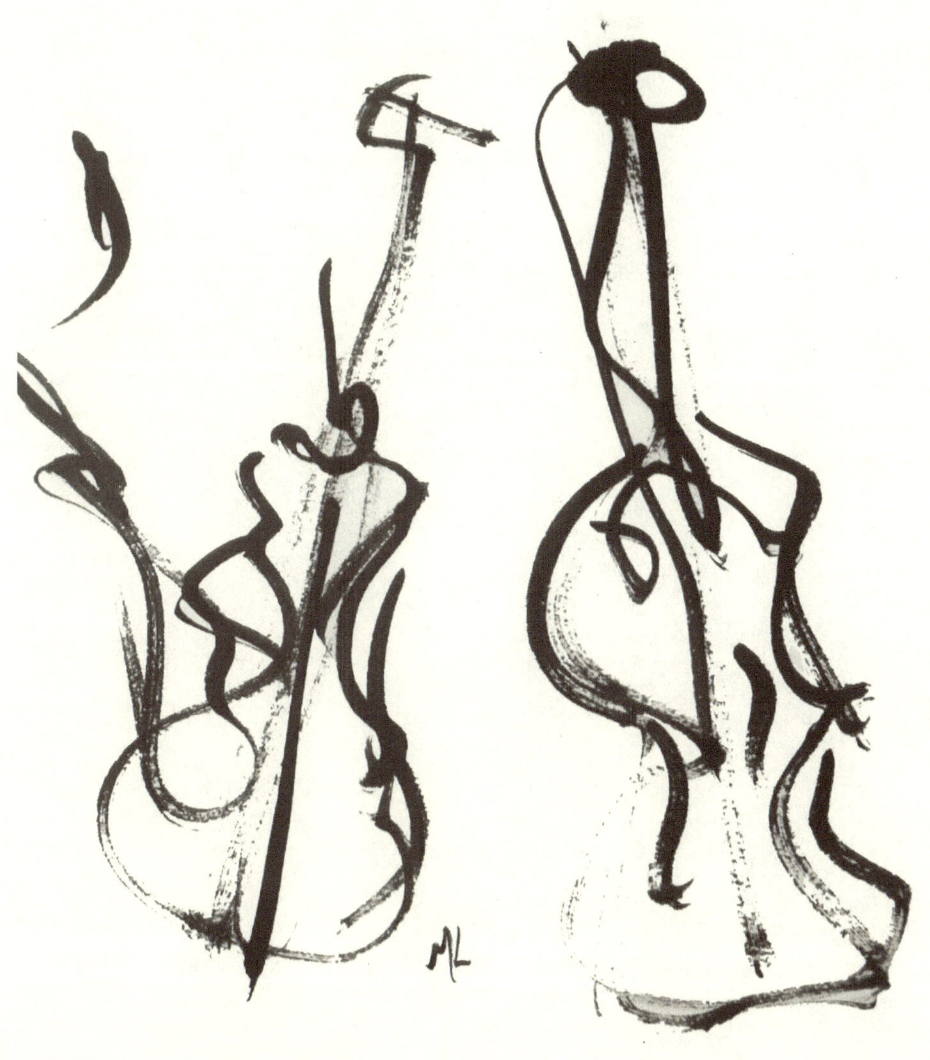

CONTENTS

Acknowledgements xi

I: Dusk Aflame

Dusk Aflame: Buenos Aires Elegy in Reverse 3
Buenos Aires Notebook: Fugues & Equivalences 21
Sizzling 43

II: Love Poems

Love Poem to Rice 47
Love Poem to Curry 48
Love Poem to Brussels Sprout 50
Love Poem to Carrot 53
Love Poem to Orange 56
Love Poem to Honey 59
Love Poem to *Media Luna* 60
Love Poem to Persimmon *(Quả Hồng)* 64
Love Poem to *Witthau Tom Yam Talay* 66

III: Sounds of Memory & Odes

The Other War 71

Quick Question 72

Ode to Sesame Seeds 73

Sounds of Memory & Sea 76

Rain on New Orleans 89

Alchemy 90

Houston Skyline 93

Galveston Time 95

IV. Autumnal Night's Dream

Midwinter in Buenos Aires 99

then to speak of the light 100

there are no maps for where we need to go 101

Particulars 102

did i ask for exhilaration of the body 106

Resonance 107

Notes 116

Biography 117

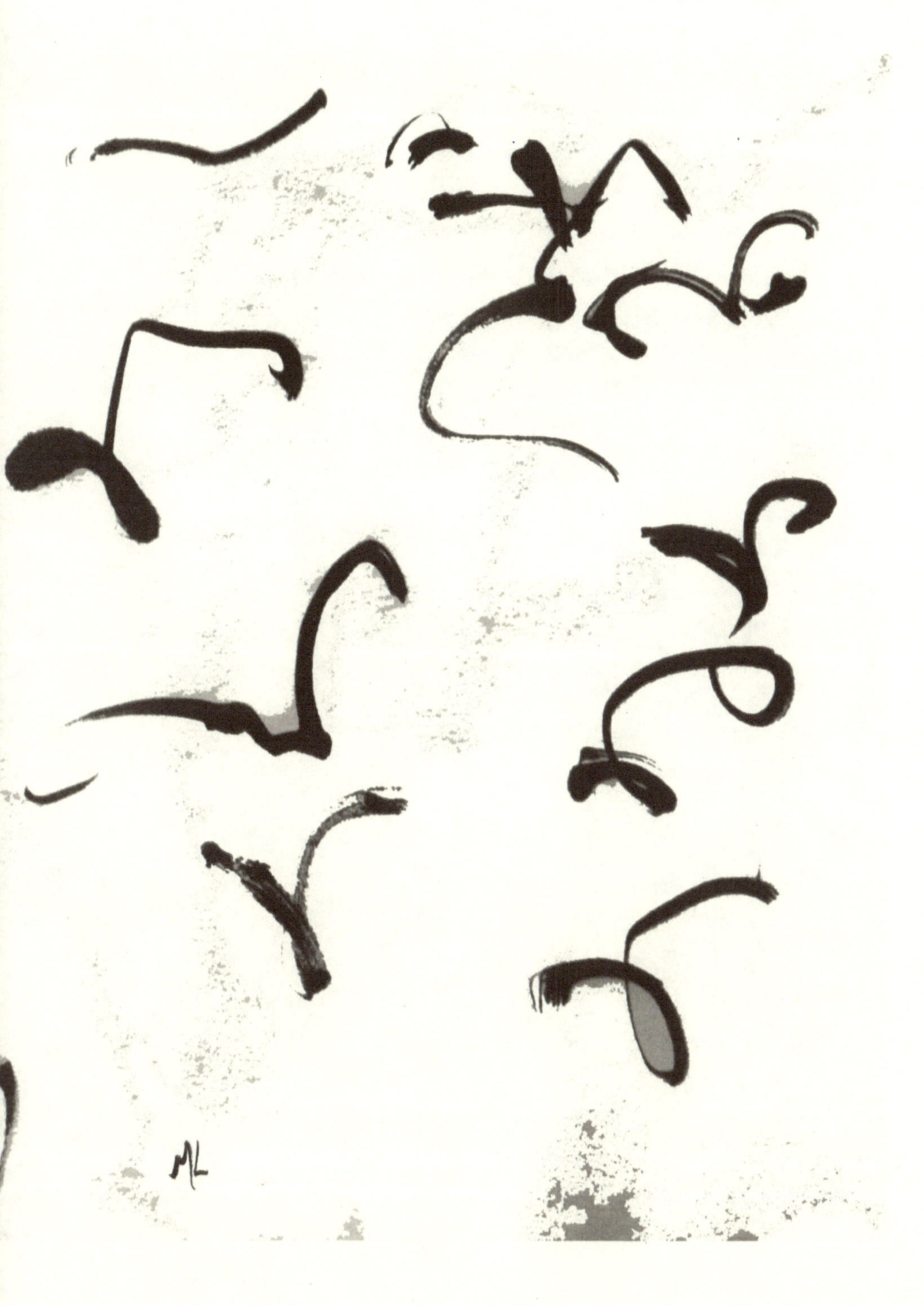

Acknowledgements

Deep gratitude to family and friends across the globe, North, South, East and West, who encouraged me, knowingly and unknowingly, in the writing and making of these poems, drawings and paintings. Special thanks to my mother, Dr. Bui Nhu; J.A.; Dr. Judith Stacey; Stephen Page.

Grateful acknowledgement to the following journals, anthologies, and their editors for first publishing these poems.

A Poetry Congeries, Connotations Press (www.connotationpress.com): "Dusk Aflame: Buenos Aires Elegy in Reverse," Sections 1-10.

*Drunken boat (*www.drunkenboat.com): "The Other War"

Hearths, An anthology: "Dusk Aflame: Buenos Aires Elegy in Reverse," Sections 11-15. (forthcoming)

Hinchas de la poesia (www.hinchasdepoesia.com): "Sounds of Memory & Sea"

The Inquisitive Eater, New School Food (inquisitiveeater.com): "Love Poem to Media Luna"; "Love Poem to Persimmons (Quả Hồng)"; "Love Poem to Curry"

The Margins, Asian American Writers' Workshop (aaww.org): "Quick question;" "Ode to Sesame Seeds"

women: migration: poetry, an anthology, Theenk Press, New York: from "Buenos Aires Notebook: Fugues & Equivalences"; "did i ask for exhilaration of the body?"; "Particulars"; "Love Poem to *Witthau Tom Yam Talay*"

DUSK AFLAME

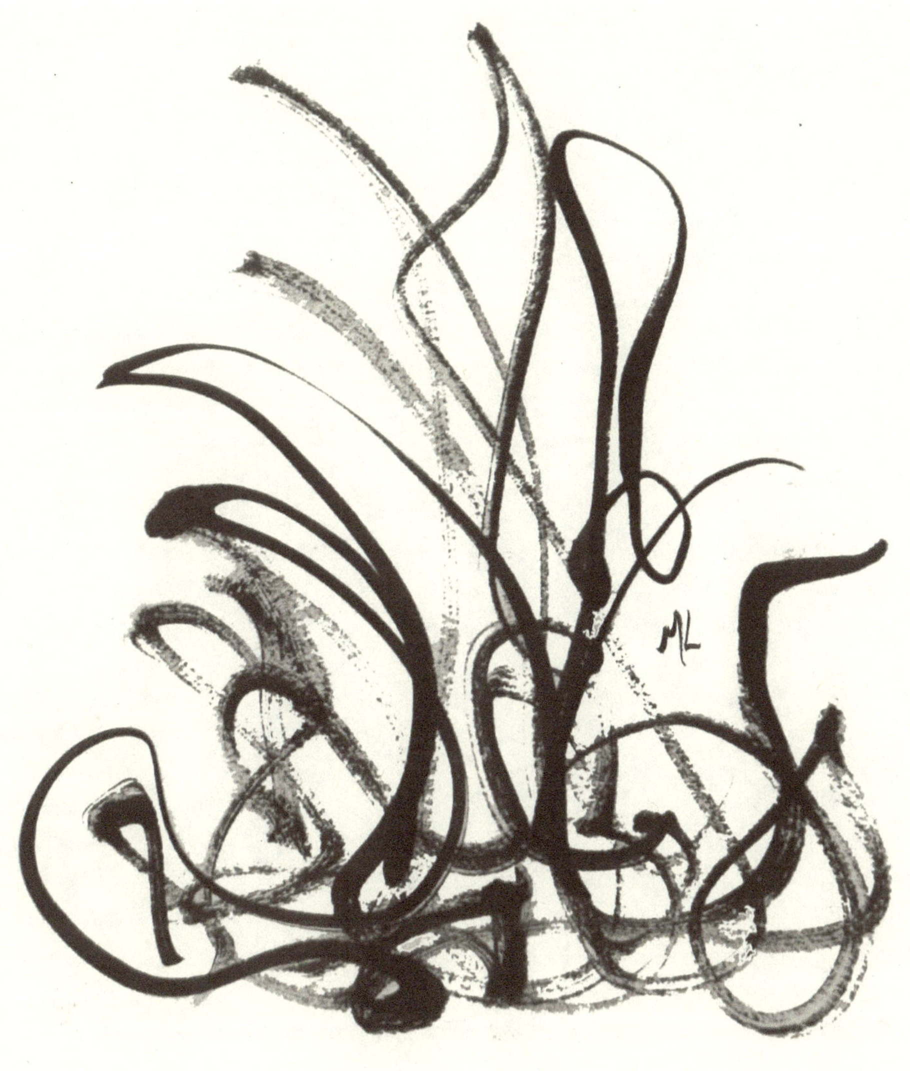

Dusk Aflame—
Buenos Aires Elegy in Reverse

prelude

Into the night

alone invisible

forfeiting all design

channel

the energies

1

the one who is afraid to fall asleep
fears death
a flicker
the last figment   invisible   the barest
of semblances
inward lotus   concealed orchid child

going at the speed of sound   talking at the speed of light thinking
at the speed of sight

every image   every creature takes your form
everything your likeness

tears flow from this strewing
flowers over the path

i breathe the air that was you
deeply   securely   breathe in your aura

fragments & bones
femur & dust
dusk   now nothing matters

2

a child disappeared   an uncle disappeared   a baby gone
the hole within grows   walking invisibles

terror   lurks
below the epidermis   all around   under the regime

people walk   ride
buses   alive

in poverty
cleaning the streets of all that they can muster

peddling everything possible   *paltas* 3 for 5 *pesos*
socks   clothes   flesh   anything

selling skin
one's insides
rumbling like ants

after the climax   what is there left to sell?

3

notice the edges of air

pitiful semblance of reality

self evaporated

only bitterness like stone

reality pinpricks

an almond nut's core

4

in the obtuse sky   no news of you
in my heart   you abide

porteños walk with pain
of disappearances

holes rippling   their hearts   walking hollow

invisible to the eye
the string that leads me to the universe

rummage amongst the dusk
of skeletons

5

the look   eyes furrowed

lovers locked thigh to thigh   lip to lip
like an animal with two hearts

two minds   two souls
realizing infinity

dizzying city   of people scurrying
lights red & neon

horizon of black   buildings
elegiac night

6

hyperventilate before entering the subway
to oxygenate the blood

grayness mobility of the moment

masses of people living for want

shades of unrest hues of bereavement

colors of a dance swirling tumultuously

in one month
everything has changed

a broken glass broken dishes

& women confined to childrearing

7

pursuing what?   an ideal
a better self

the city
swept up   rising with the winds

crystal light   vital energy
a mind that opens flowerlike   embracing

all-knowing

immediately evanescent
glows from knowing

8

the desperate & needy
beaten down with nothing
(with nothing we have come into this world
& with nothing we go)

collecting dust viruses
autumns spring fast cars pollution ornate architecture

deaths come faster & faster now
veering at a startling rate like torn leaves souls flying up

women carrying

men & boys tying up cartons recyclables
grey figures moving along the dark streets
combustion of the city

9

the darkening

colectivos all night

blazing neon trails but which bus goes from here to there?

which goes to you my love?

which to your bewildered

heart?

10

Buenos Aires aflame

goes into fall

twelve *chicas* for every *chico*   ten *chicos* for every *chica*

plurality invites freedom

in falling   i ascend to my heights

in letting go   i gain everything

(yet

nothing works   nothing's on time

everything staggers   sputters   heats up

agitated)

11

Crossing a bridge of rotted wood
graffiti   quick feet   trains   the heart overbeating

a wide berth   brown air
air that passes   that goes nowhere
then settles   grey   swirling breathless air

in *Once*   boys & girls sit on school steps after school
grain dissolves   graininess

the taxi driver says, "*no te distraís   caminá   suerte* "

i clutch my bag   & fearlessly
walk across the bridge to sing

12

Neon night   squash   tomatoes   fires

sirens come

spiraling

exhaust   the exhausted   have exhausted everything
on *Corrientes* a dirty
griminess pervades

foliage   trees   a respite from this hard of breath
hard of hearing

a city in sync with its own disorder & chaos

grimness of carnivores
a night   in squares   rectangles

night in which you are in my rays   my heart
night of stings

translucent dealings wings in water

dry kisses on hair

13

Write as if falling
while falling
the grandest gesture

to breathe   breathless
underwater   inhaling the ocean

Dusk with her many proportions   full of identities
pregnant with dawn
with an idea of Earth

night enters
as a sigh   then   *molto lento*
aphoristic calls

this evanescence   a fluorescent hummingbird

14

this daze   by   width of mind   stretch

of landscape

like the first notes of a melancholy tune

the first strikes of murky

death

was it the shriek & shrill of a bird

or something else?

how did we put time to it?

15

when Dusk transforms herself   she's utterly light
her soul had taken up most of the space in her body
unawares i gather the density
of her diaphanous body
her soul   already flown

the dream this life:
floating   i walk slowly
to a rhythm of the ethereal
& tango-colored music

unsuspected
you usher   in clear as the day   & water
as eyes

begin again
associate with only air & music

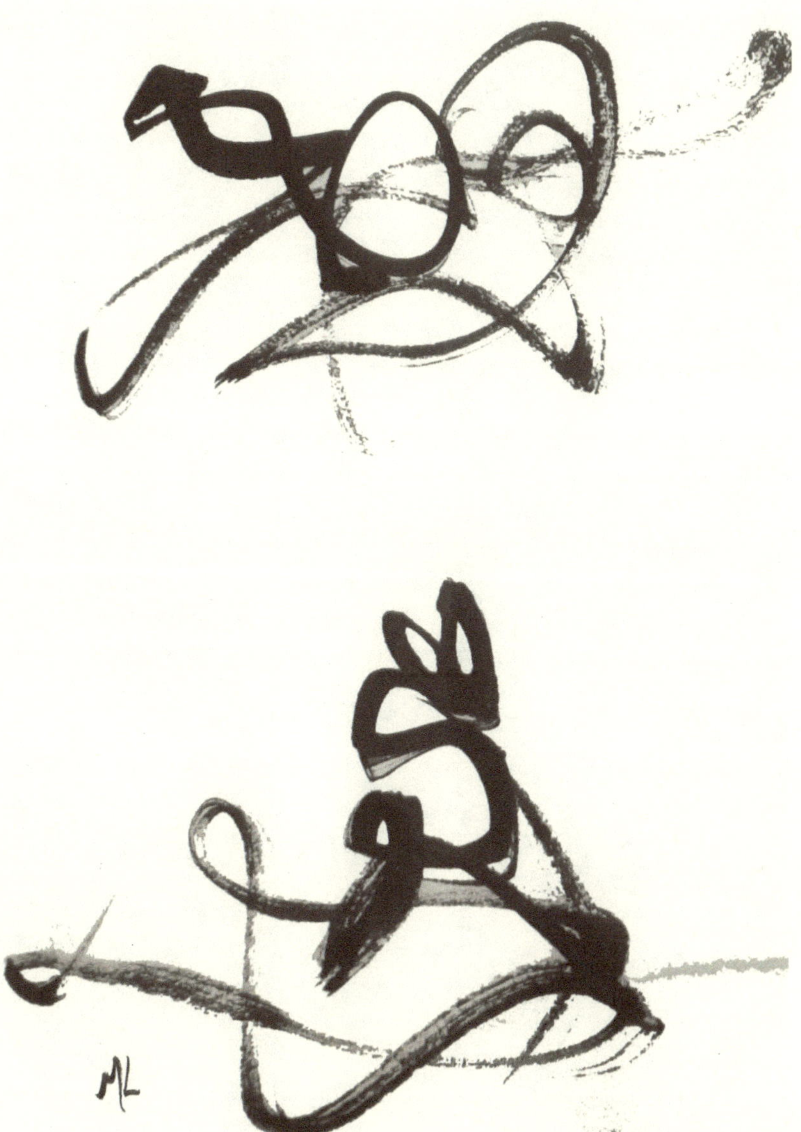

Buenos Aires Notebook:
Fugues & Equivalences

1

an owl's flight   peerless
swooping   swerving in a silver array of wisdom
fastidious to silence

city of dreams
city of dreamlessness
city of sleeplessness   & waking while sleeping
sleeping while awake

city of the comatose
ciudad de los muertos
city of remorse   failed & light-hearted
romances
city in which your nightmares follow you
in which your dreams abandon you
or in which you abandon your dreams
in which most is impossible   without shouting

sleeping   i awaken knowing
my waking thoughts keep dreaming
of possibilities
& keep on working

2

[*head down*   *don't look to see what people are doing*]

ciudad de lluvia   remorseless   unrelenting

rain that augurs   decay   destruction

the clearing of all social events   all afternoon teas

work   all obliterated

except for Nisman's silent march

people somber in umbrellas

un sueño:

mammoth elephants their sleek silver trunks

dead on the ground

flat silvery-white with sweat

prostrate no longer in agony

trunk down

in utter morbidity   i move forward closing my eyes

blind myself

cuaderno de Buenos Aires

dirt   water   & turmoil

& oh   pls listen to this song

as we die   as we go forth

& as never before make sense

of our lives

3

make sense of our lives as we dying awake

sing the songs

whisper the remnants

of life into each other's ears

last year's *zapatos y guitarras*

thrown out symbols with long arms

political assassinations tire me

cerca de la muerte

leaves come together form a book by themselves

leaflets jump become more than

themselves

lily-fly season

& how had i forgotten that it takes 2 to tango

the poor the mad roam the streets

echoed by the horses' clop clop

the folks begging for *cartón & papel*

begging for paper & recyclables

daily depressions

give me a hand out, will ya?

4

horses traverse the streets of Buenos Aires take away trash
decorated horses in parks take customers for rides

(remember the elephants in Bangkok begging
heat in which fungus festers)

down today into the cellar of my thoughts
beg for my thoughts
get in line with everything
strengthen myself mis pies

the old recycled the new newly won

¿qué debemos saber?
without our own thoughts without butter
olive oil
sweet potatoes
Apollo's strumming

5

un día con lluvia calorosa

how i must defer death to the dying
how i must forgive & go on
how i must not retreat   but go forth   *adelante*

even on *Corrientes*
& *Córdoba*
& all the streets in between
how i must refrain from talking about politics
or they will stab me with their words & looks

yet what is more important than talking about how we
live our lives?

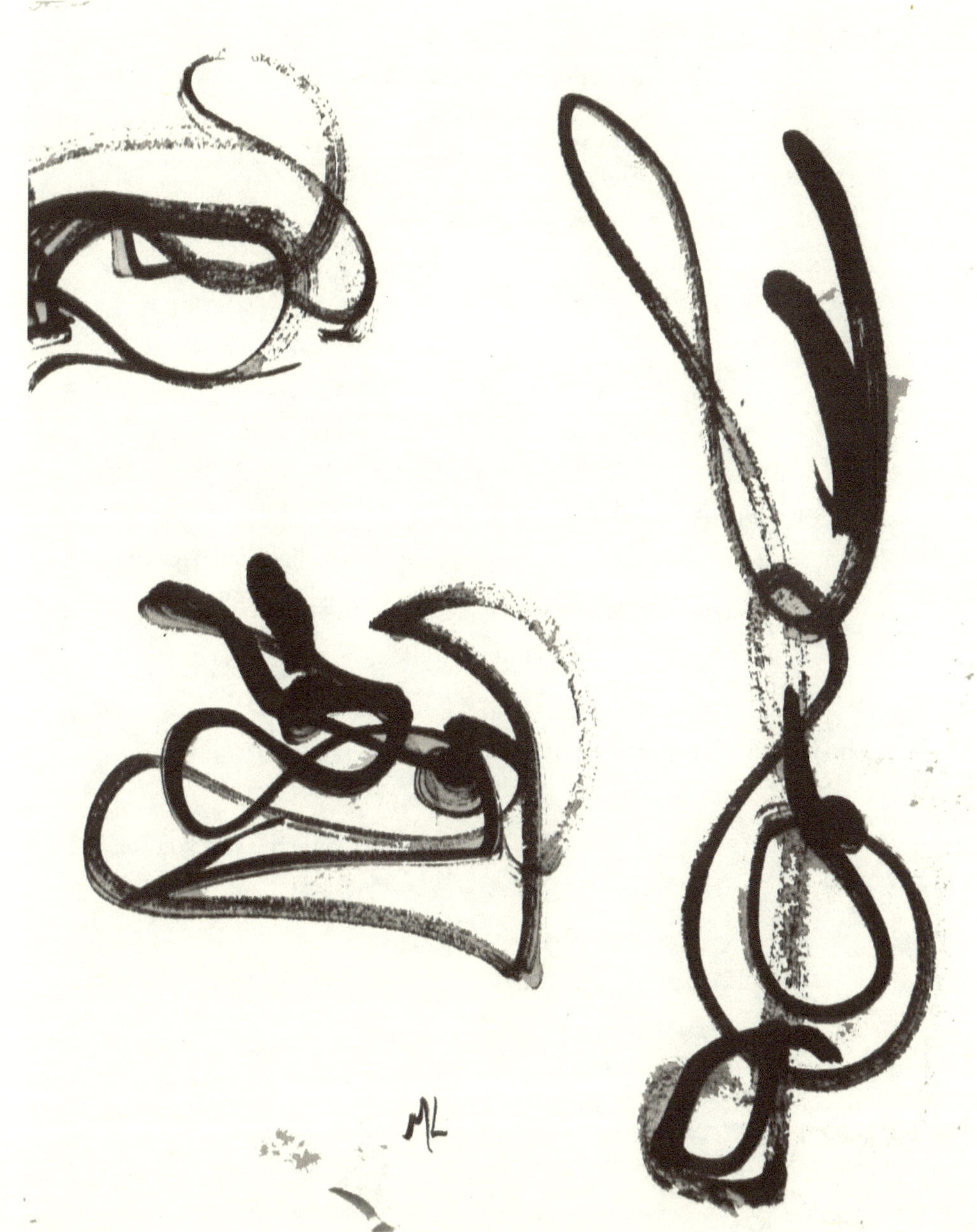

6

Corrientes windswept
hordes of people & *panaderías*

hot bus scalding wind
let the energy
open up your chest

the *bandoneón's*
e minor chord like a dolorous cool stream
over one's fingers striking the buttons
to let the chord's light fall over you
to let one's being absorb the many-densities
of sound

exhilaration of creation
i've come
to remember you the way you were

7

the *bandoneón's* gush like a bloodstream flush
resonant   then dissipating
delivering
a world of opposites

for one cannot exist without its opposite
a baleful of killings   one more horrifying than the next

too terrified to go out
to tell

death for a dollar
a dollar for a death

desire for the truth
to know what happened
to speak one's mind

you let in the light of ten thousand trees
a million nights dressed in shade
into the harbor of pity
& you will be thus & thusly
as you were born

10

the shade of one thousand trees awaits you
slaughter of bleak time
in the laughter of darkness
police swimming in their suits & cries

to speak or not speak
to die or not to go on

words like horses galloping
a fever of words
in the forever of words
upon waking

dance of delirium
string of words
relentless understanding perpetual forgetting
my willingness to understand & be understood

awash in the trash
relentless that sweeping all of us
tension & release
birds of many feathers flocking

11

unzipping the universe

letting go

i have desired eons & now no more

i invite the multitudes to come to my doorstep

the great voices

#18F

they have marched in silence

chanting wait in the rain protest quietly

with their signs

260,000 people waiting in the rain

as if for a bus #18F

for change waiting for change for homage

with the signs *"llora para mi Argentina"*

while rain falls on the *Plaza de Mayo*

everything dies

& renews by itself

ah

& nothing is everything at once

12

en un "país absurdo" (dice una mujer argentina)

where effort doesn't get you ahead

thinking

doesn't necessarily help

and *la suerte* has everything to do with it

how much have i lost

how much has one lost

a day

several years

in the vanished night a ship of nights

disappeared

a river & ten thousand years

my forest of thoughts

days thriving on savage darkness

a day gained in thurberian thought

for its own sake

i wanted to know

the nectar

13

the miles to go before i walk
the pudding step
                    a liquid dance more than is asked for

where to find rice flour in Buenos Aires?   for *Tết*   the New Year
what to bring back from eternal thirst?
                                        bright endeavors

what to nourish
                    what to remember
                                        what to wash away

memories revisited
                    thrown down   thrashed   throttled   still born
the casualties

        i left   i keep on leaving
                & the name i saw in my dream   came to me in real life

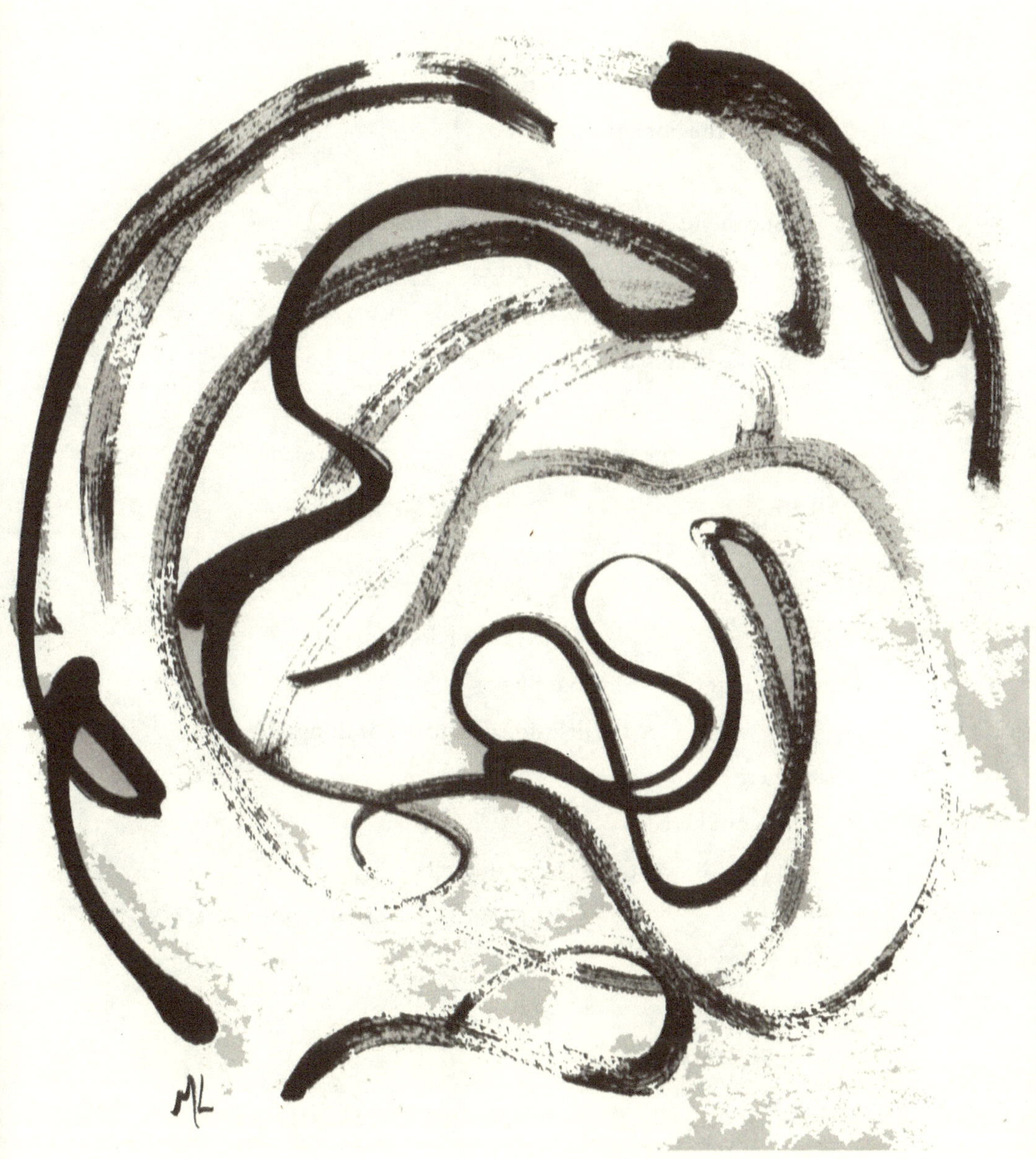
ML

14

the signature was there   of the heavens scribbled
    then   the horrors unveiled

then came the real person   one year later
  from the melody   then the dancer

first came the imagination   the voice

            the lotus   a thing of the present
evolving
      always of the present

                 what have i done?
i have thought of nothing but plants
             & the delusionary quality of things
what is here
      is not here
          & what is there   matters
                         can one not matter?

15

not the light this life not this urban
ditty not this waking world

the lotus sits still
buildings will burn
an apocalypse of the highest order
should one die
& leave with no remorse?
an apocalypse of the oldest disorder

leave with no remorse

all your images to last
yes this the image function & life

the forever data & a forever
life in the eternal
socket of desire

hard drive of hope

give me a dash of decency

16

a line   blue as the waves of your depression

where did we hope to go?

where did we go to hope?

what did we hope to do?

in the forever world

of here

what was gone   is gone   will be gone

what was here   is here   will be here

your hair

disappears into a thin line

on the horizon

17

un día sin vos

once believing & then the disbelief

the status quo reigns
in this dreamless city
of armpits legs high heels
a dreamy city of European architecture
dilapidated

(Egypt & the drifting sands of the pyramids
the Muslim men there who followed me around
& my parents upset
roving sands)

what are we to know
without our own thoughts without butter
olive oil sweet potato
your nemesis
your own lover your *matador*
everything awash on the shores of Jupiter

18

being that we have forgotten what to do

what will we say   & how will we say it?

what tangos will we sing?   for whom?

what is poetry for you?

then to express the inexpressible

the untamable

with eyes shut   heart hemorrhaging

hands numb

feet barely moving

through a city as if blind

feeling one's way in the wind   rain & dirt

let the mind move

through the still mind

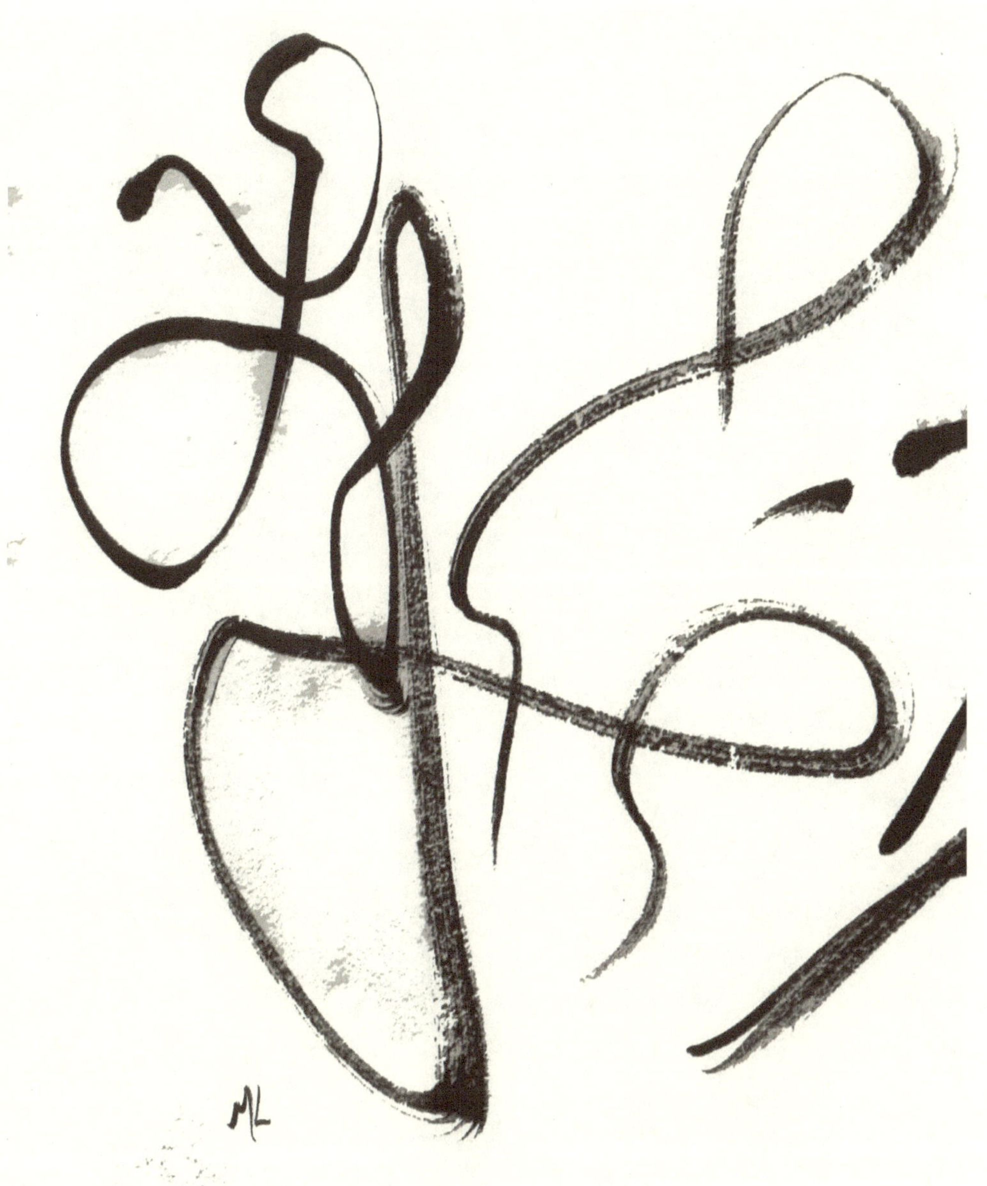
ML

Sizzling

1

Hot says the city   ssssizzzzling
glide over me
the river's voice croons "stay with me   i will make you new"

does your lust have an object? does your love have an object?

2

i hate C. (who is C?)   —all those men.

i hate Pinkerton.

i detest winter, Buenos Aires in winter. i hate men running after me in the streets howling for sex.

other things i abhor: jealous women   yellow leaves falling.

being away from home. i find exes intolerable, meeting exes, especially exes with whom you had been with for too too long.

having coffee after a *milonga.* i detest men who are in a hurry. kisses half done, sex half done. i abhor quick sex.

missing people, as if a part of me had died with them. as if they had kept a part of me, & i am not whole without them.

weak women. i despise Madame Butterfly.

the day after having sex quickly. loving someone so much & they only want you for sex.

men who are jerks, *boludos, pelotudos.*

how has it gotten to this?

3

what i love

giving birth to the music

feeling it all come from my fingers   like invisible twine weaving

magically

II

Love Poems

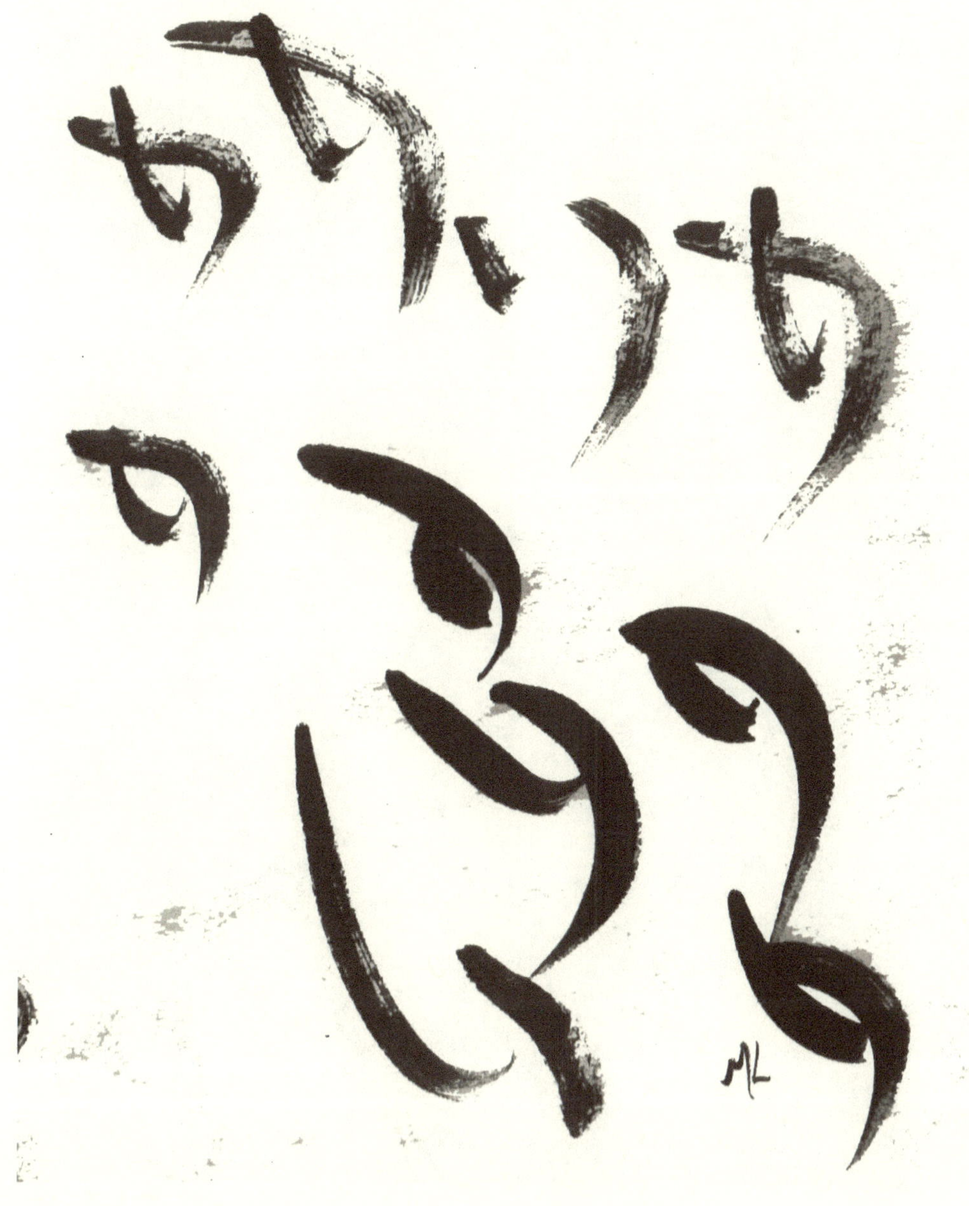

Love Poem to Rice

O glamourless ordinary rice

i hardly even think of you   taking you for granted

blandly   you drone
white brown red
& shades in between
a constant love

from the terraces and steppes   from the partitioned
fields
unhusked

young strapling

life wouldn't be a life without you

Love Poem to Curry

but the promise of a moment

of spices   luxurious   uncontainable

how will i remember your embrace?
how will i remember your trem-
bling?

how will i remember your presence around me
all-enveloping?

i only need to taste you slowly   daily

origins rich as sand

your powers   multifaceted   gingerly   i savor
your ingenuity

what are you?

mysterious   complex   luscious   dark
as if behind velvet curtains   closed doors
satiny as the Sahara   as your turmeric

breathless   as ever you make me

in the spices of your delirium

turmeric   coriander   fenugreek   fennel
ginger   cloves   garlic   curry leaves
peppers   chilies   mustard

endless varieties of you
seamless steamy concoctions
fragrant
as the years are long
as the years   terse

that unfurls centuries   thousands of years   knowledge

traditions glowing   of temples   robes flowing orange
rich dark past
of desire   of uncountable kisses
or kisses missed

Love Poem to Brussels Sprout

Wild miniature cabbage

leafy green buds   curly wings   everything in miniature

of the gemmifera group of cabbages   *brassica oleracea*

sensualist   sensationalist   clustered on your highfalutin stalks

hard shell on the outside   & inside   bitter   dense

wrapped up in your own destiny

you need nobody   but your own self

i can only love you on the surface   not knowing what you are inside

tough stratums of you

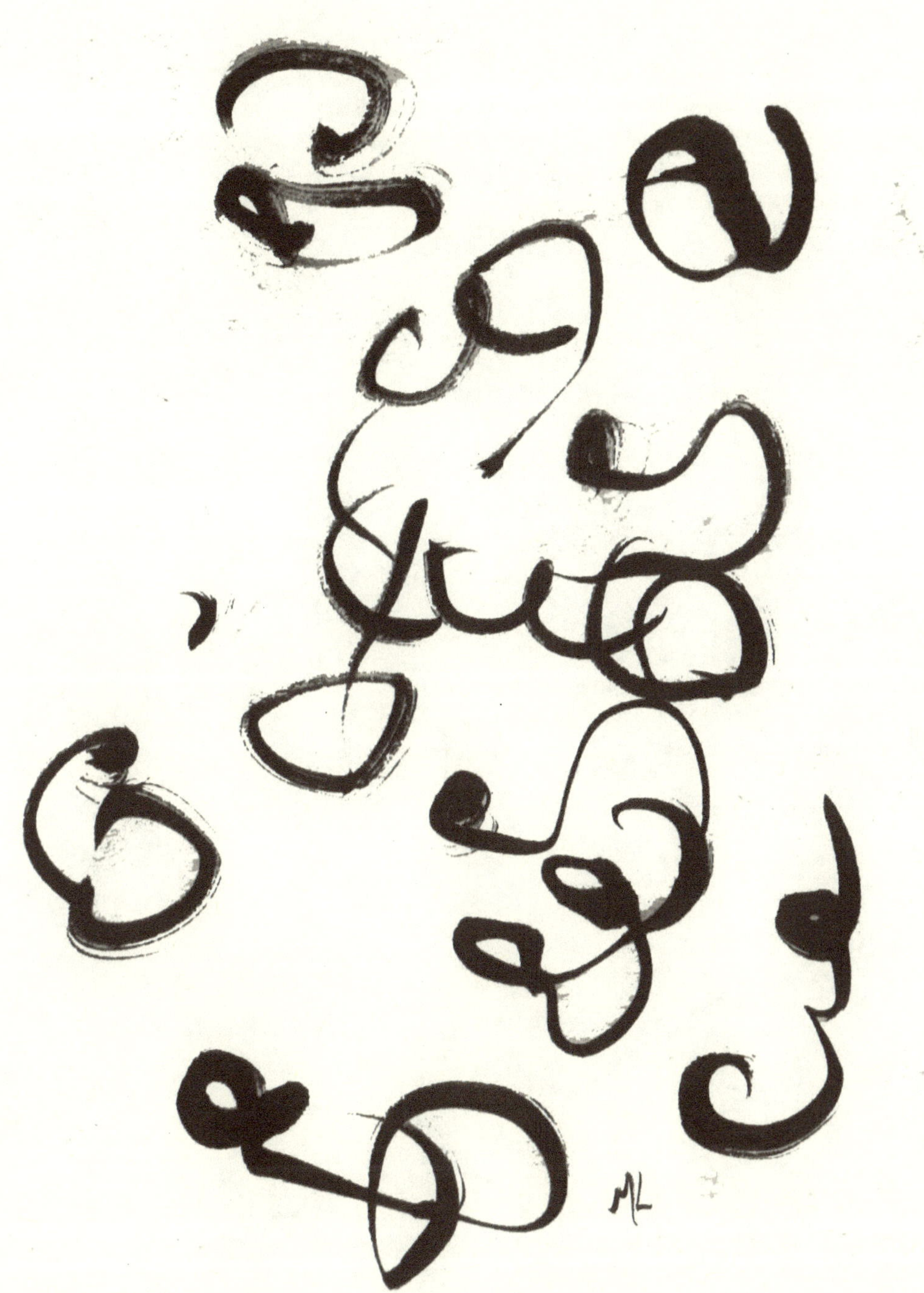
ML

Love Poem to Carrot

Tangy colored   beta-carotene

sliced another way   down its length   staff of life
sliced across   eye for the better
eye of the beloved

ground-grown affinities with soil   selenium rich

oracular   faithful
as we should be to the earth

color of my uterus
crunch
density of orange
flavonoid opaque soul
a voice   clear   pregnant with yearning

(your obscure qualities   *anthelmintic   carminative*
contraceptive   deobstruent diuretic   emmenagogue galactogogue
ophthalmic   stimulant   oedema   not to be forgotten)

julienned to eat with my favorite Vietnamese dishes

your immense orangatan color

dear carrot

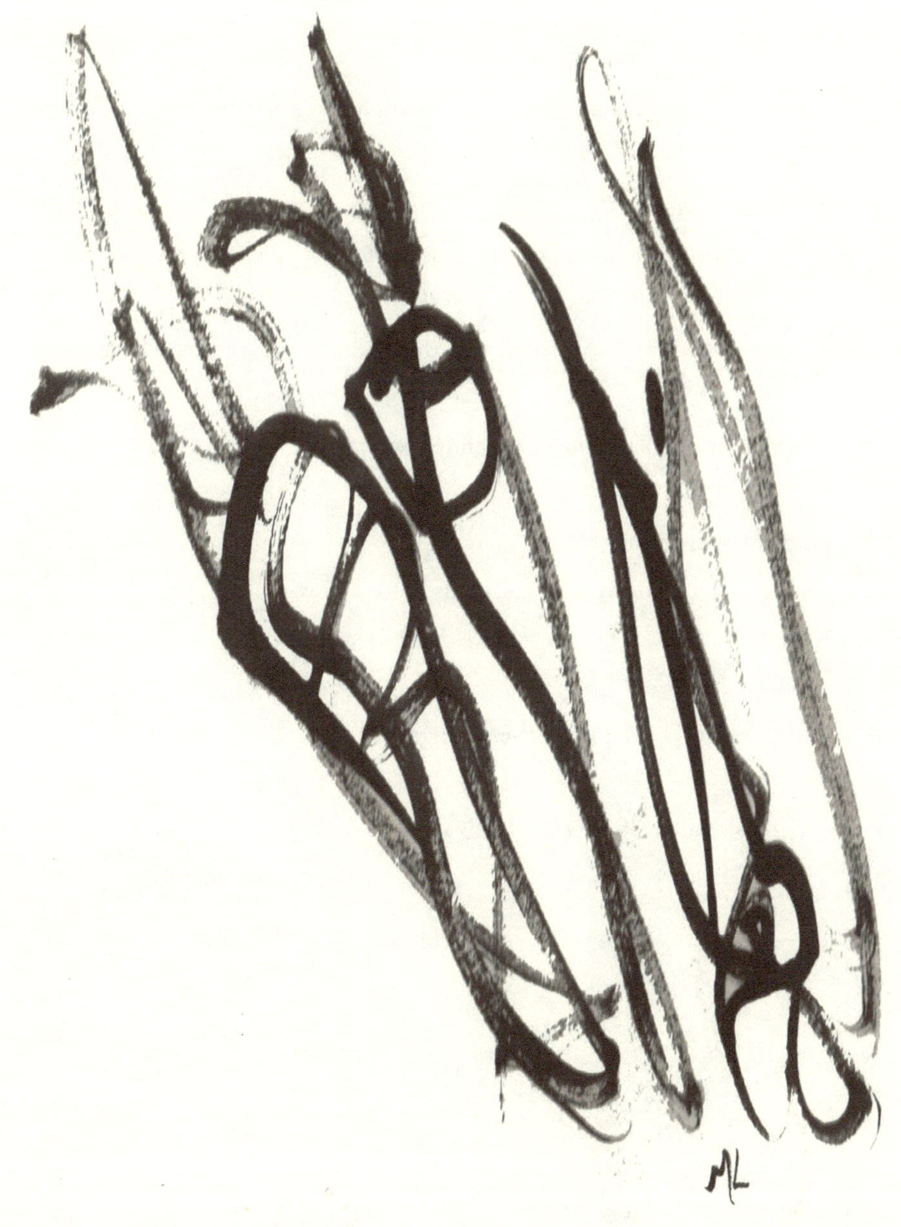

Love Poem to Orange

Orbital orange of my nights   my deliverance

an orange *exprimido*   a full glass of you
packages of sweetness   memory in division

planetary diversions   sectioned heart

the soul's memory   of tender sweetness

fulcrum of creativity
into sections i sense you   slowly

yet eating you is quick
gulp   low A   then a higher octave

sultriness that sings of exotic lands
fruit-laden vibrant

robust

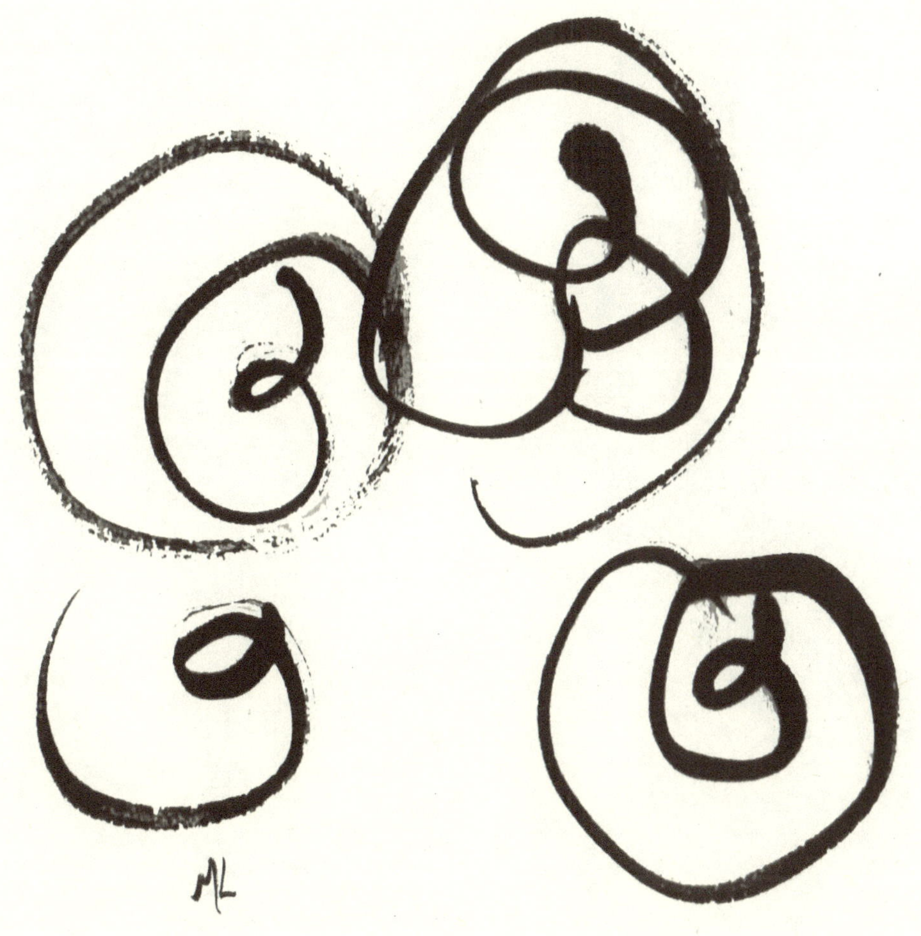

Love Poem to Honey

The more i sing of your loveliness   the more i am in tune with life
golden as candlelight
emblem of life   swirling bees
thicker than blood
i scoop you into my teas & coffees

anti-bacterial   you fortify my poor throat from colds
to sing more highly of your loveliness

i dive everyday into your thick sea   amber serum

resilient   never self-effacing   your brilliance shines through
with every taste   with every drop

on my tongue   your flexible body
serum of life
pure   delectable   best organic
liquid gold

Love poem to *Media Luna*

It didn't take me long to fall for you

what the ethereal eye beholds
in ascension
half moon crescent earth

O *media luna*
de manteca

my secret sin that i devour whenever
durante las noches sueño de tu
cuerpo
tender
feathery body waiting for me

(yet really wanting to forget you)

how easily you break away
into lithe fibers the way i break
away from this life
you melt in my mouth *dos ríos*
en un desierto

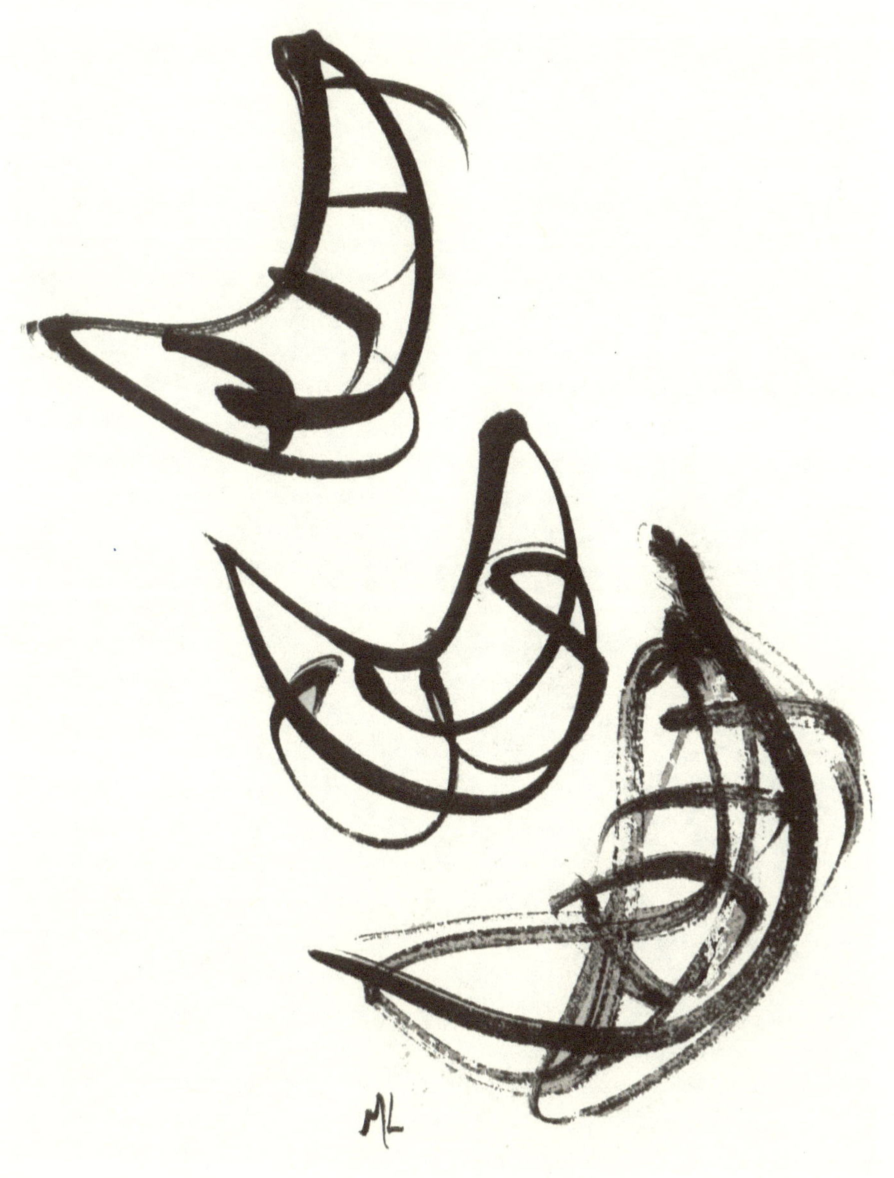

una media luna
crossing   une croissante   en el cielo

rising when the sun sets

swathed in sublime butter light

delectable crust   warm interior   fazing into air
del orno

mi boca en tu boca
mis ojos en tus ojos

how easily you give way to your precious inside
how your wings fly effortlessly

in my favorite café in Buenos Aires   you come in threes
cada una   delicada como
el rocío de la mañana

each an imperfect half moon

Love Poem to Persimmon (*Quả Hồng*)

Smooth-skinned   orange interior   exterior
heart-shaped
your pull more intense than gravity
adamant kiss wet on wet
textures in-between

your sweetness croons   of days
in Việt Nam   those simmering Texas days   mother's
varieties of *hồng*
from her garden   crunchy & silken
those Tokyo 東京 days
diligently on branches
during December in Japan you sway

leisurely turning snow to fire
you turn as the earth's axis does
imperceptibly
adorning skeletal trees
like a design for a new brimmed hat
mid-winter snow dusts your curves
orange

feverish thoughts

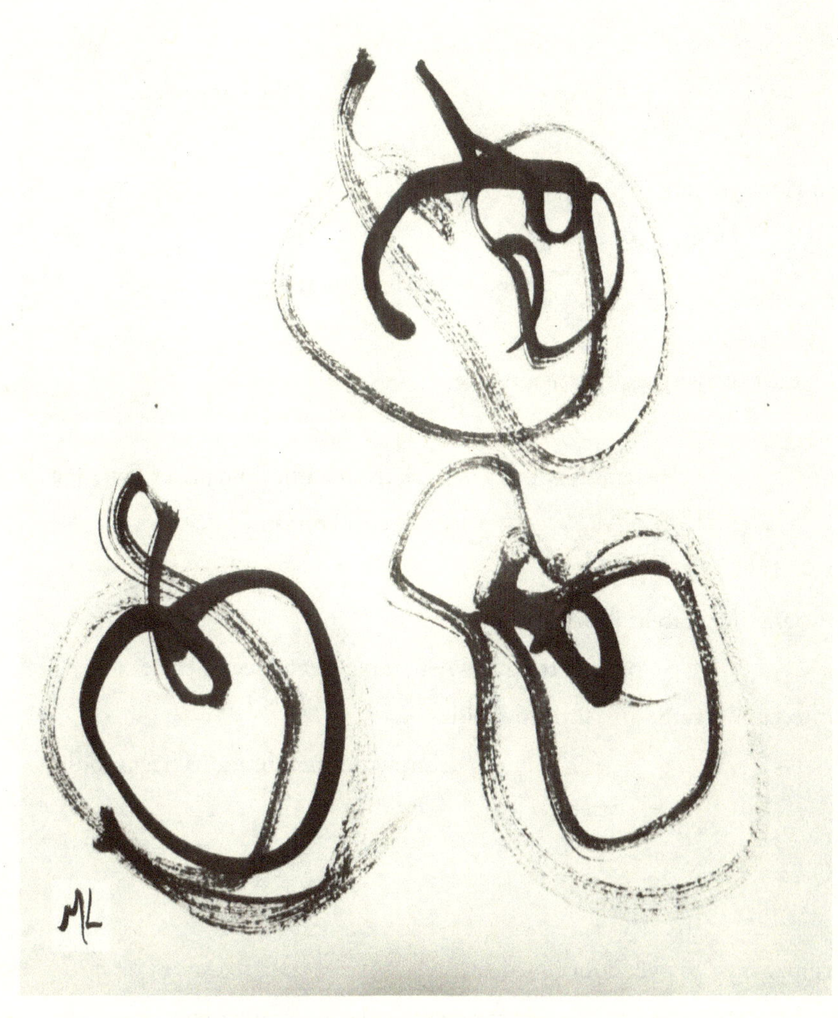
ML

Love Poem to *Witthau Tom Yam Talay*

i stare into you   O my *Tom Yam*

your beauty   difficult to behold
i will never be the same again

so saucy you are
tangy   your body
limed with a halo of orange & red

let me taste you again & again

lemon grass   galangal   fresh kaffir lime juice   fish sauce
fresh chilli onions

angular crab limbs
put my tongue where it has never been before
into your caverns   shrimpy spine
slurp your membranous rice noodles

O *Tom Yam*

i graze my lips over your lime leaves
suck on your stalks of lemon grass
hold the slivers of ginger

over my tongue

your tongues of red chilli peppers tantalize me

in Bangkok you reign supreme
after you
i am not the same

let me taste you again
& again
your marrow

III

Sounds of Memory & Odes

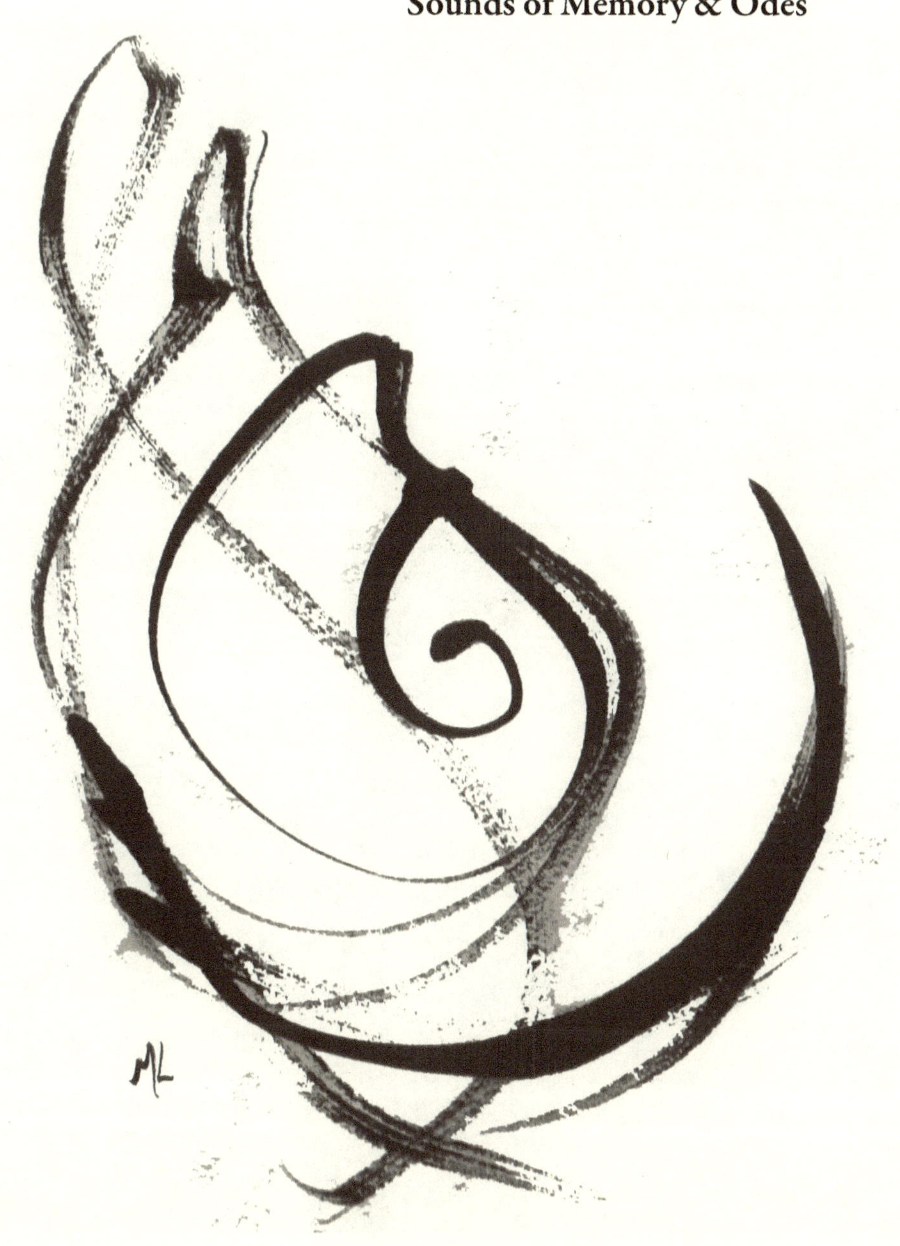

The Other War

a wall still exists in us brought on by the war   fences us in

still it slithers created many decades ago by everyone around me that
suffers

high long & vertiginous   delusional blocking everything in its path

not forgiving   the wall demands all eyes on it   demands blood

a mental wall of steel dirt brick

bleeding   a partition of paranoia that does not let
the other in

a barricade of eyes red & blue

still continues walls us in

& all the abortions

Quick Question

Action in lies
          no action without lies

is there life   — inside
these bones is there life in not-editing?

                              darling i am without you
                    i am with you

everywhere it is blossoming

a liver a life lived
through the sieve
                    are you mine?
          or do you have many   lovers?

there it is   i've said it
in more ways than one
there it is   the glue holding everything together
                                        not a mistake

how you moved your hair bursting over your shoulders
                                        a spray of water
                                   & how you held me

Ode to Sesame Seeds

in my quietude   i see you vast   far ranging   springing out

abundant   grainy   diverse   benne *sesamum indicum*

internal yet   outwardly basking in sun

inside thousands of thoughts spring   thousands of your seeds
that bring to thought

purposeful   with your many purposes

i sprinkle your seeds on rice   everything i eat

how to endure time
without your nourishing seeds?

how to be clear as the earth   without clinging to sand?
flowing through my hands like water

one seed clings to my palm

darling

atom   spinning   sterling   you are a teardrop

i shower you on rice sprinkle you soy sauce in salads sautés

will i completely understand your filamentous
yearning pouring forth?
a desert without water without you
sands of sesame seeds all about us

your kisses the oasis where
my soul drinks

your caresses the waves
where i swim trying to find myself

in memory
of your caresses i find you a single seed

Sounds of Memory & Sea

1

you an eagle
fiercely

streaked silver

early morning
the jungle's whiskers bristle

(the Andaman Sea)

2

the human body is perfect   for walking running lovemaking
if loved well   we will live forever

resplendent as the baritone blue sea

indestructible a centenarian oak   an undecipherable crystal
unparalleled in vigor   persuasive
as a typhoon

luminosity

3

an island

the balmy air

i swim alone

but for a tiny crab

alongside

i wake to tell of the dream

do waves tire

the waves of your hand?

4

the turquoise waters blue as eyes   iridescent trees exfoliate energy

cliffs higher than churches tall as skyscrapers

a bird crows macaws multi-colored fly over coast hinterland
to see what is underneath   gaining momentum to move forward

merge   your electricity mine
inhaling the freshness of the jungle
ocean water the sea splashing our souls
awake
we are ourselves in the translucent white
sand diaphanous blue   under aquama-
rine
skies in salt water drawing
energy from the world giving it
back

5

cats here are angular famished

birds strut proud of their prints

cicadas drone in brown & green scales

the magnolias' scent cracks open the two worlds

a sparrow   parrots   a black butterfly

on a cliff that climbers have died for

a leaf drops   at the hint of a thought

waves   all night

6

crystal-like wait for the signs receive energy from plants & sun speak the language of cats & tortoises lizards & rain clouds & leaves the language of moons & stars dragon's wings & their shadows

7

sickle moon   midpoint in the sky

sun in the east   limestone cliffs
right & left

the sea   lucid blue-green
tepid waters

8

the ocean escapes the world the world escapes to her she is a gigantic mouth that swallows boats people sand octopuses sharks fish of all nationality arms & feet by her civilization floats or drowns the lucky few who listen to her survives

9

a fetal flower you enter

like a dragon

you fly

the sound of memory

outlasts water

10

amber scales   tooth & enamel   fitting perfectly

you are silky   purposeful   thighs laterally efficient

navel against navel

11

between seasons

shifting

nightly waves

stir coconuts to lift

& fall

a spathe   & stillness

12

sea silence   jungle silence   heart silence   plethora of wills
submerged in silence

hum of silence distilled in a vat disorderly secretions silences of others' lovemaking

sage silence of stone & crystals   slow silence of candlelight   silence of roses   ants sleeping silence of palm protecting coconut   silence of your lips

silence of the moment after

13

the distance between us measured

by balsam breaths

by vibrations in our veins

coursing

14

for days we listen to the jungle's breathing i listen to yours   you
listen to mine

listen to the breathing of plants planets   solar systems

sparrows & crows come & go—where do they come from   where do
they go? ducks from which country? which hemispheres?

listen to my heart its tides beating   *listen*

15

the veil
of a mosquito net
admitting a mosquito
limestone cliffs   a climber scales

under net
the promise
of your nectar
water bellows   over-running

16

the first
& last
re-
membering

~Krabi, Thailand

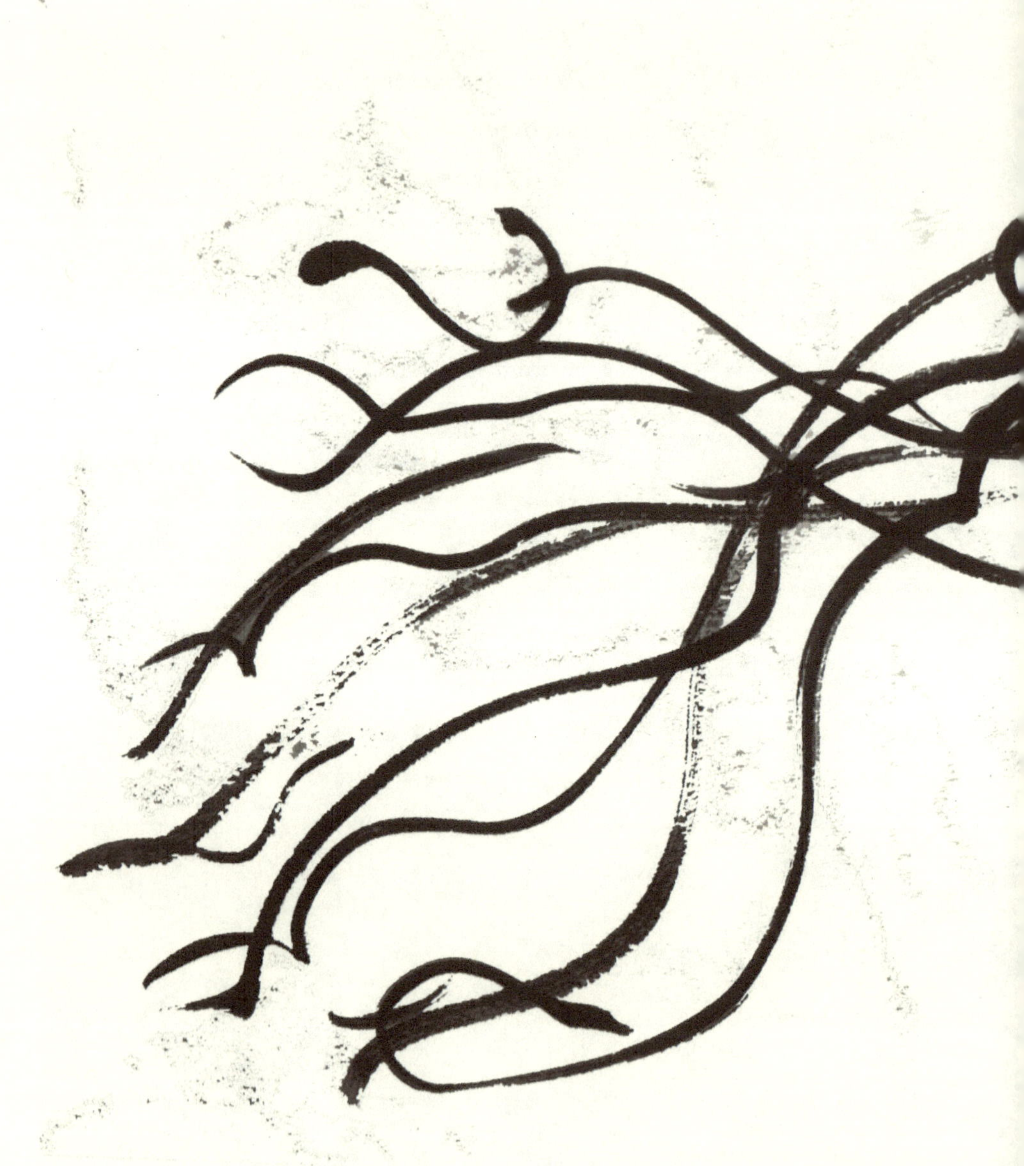

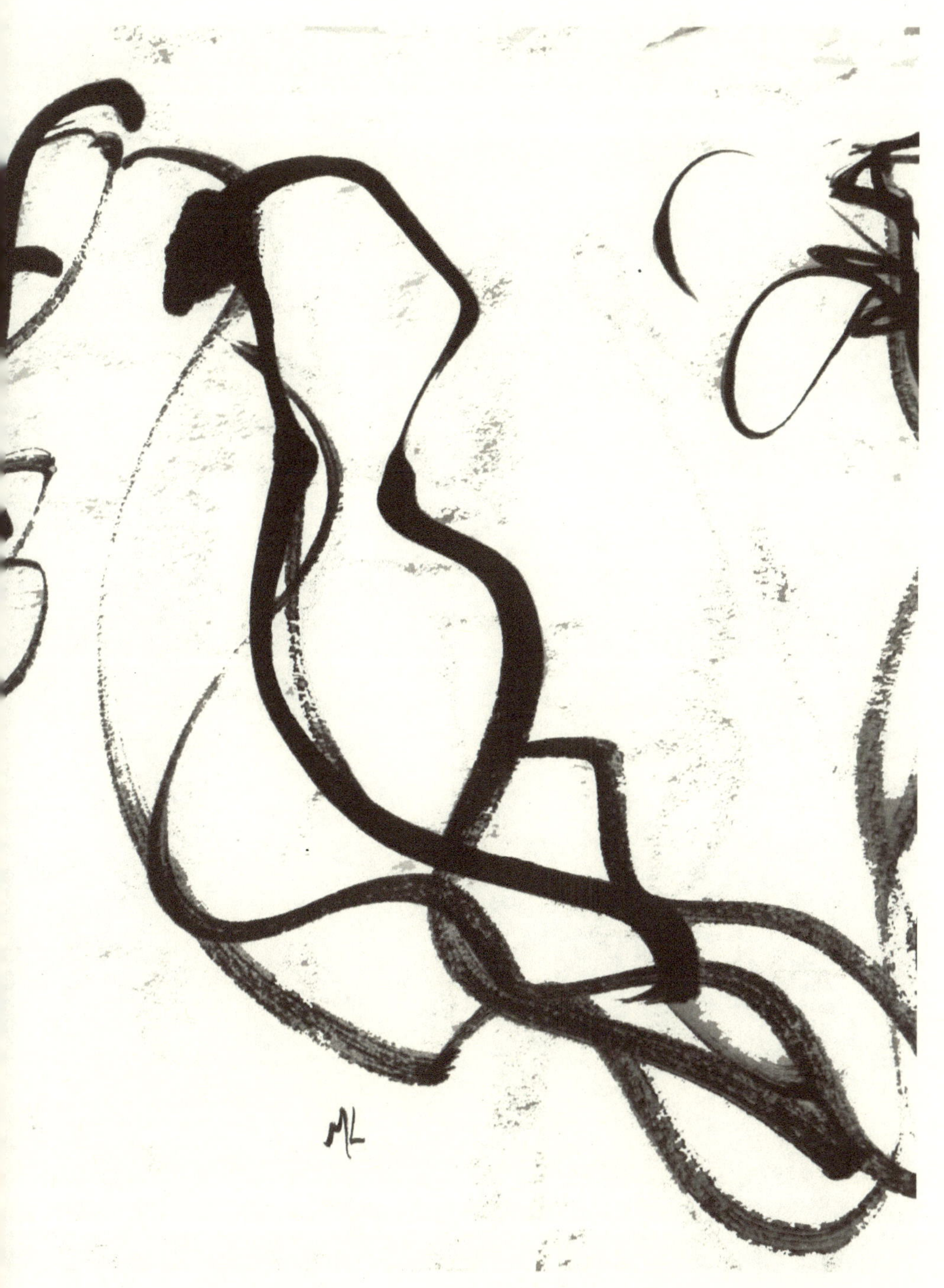

Rain on New Orleans

On the boughs
in the eaves continuous silence of rain
reining my heart
delirium of
skin against heart
where love lies
of adventures
spirals leading
the ultimate

dancing perfectly
knowing everything that one needs to know

diving with & dolphin suit
divining
divers too flesh out the fluid core

of ocean threshing
moments of resplendence
of forgiveness
of craziness ripe
bright sun dappling through trees
angels' trumpeting yellow

Alchemy

as if in a Shakespearean play
a new mode
of existence   in a nonlinear
orbit
half-awake   dreaming state
sound of blade on ice
crosses dimensions   past present & future

hand-written letters of orange & blue
blossom notes
promise
of slow bantering caresses

a blue crab crawls over the sand
a certain wispy melody wafts
over the Mississippi
over wooden planks washes over our toes
a coffer a coiffure of orchids
roses daylilies
sent dancing from New Orleans

sounds our hearts

a street full of jazz stored in the air

plays to those who would listen

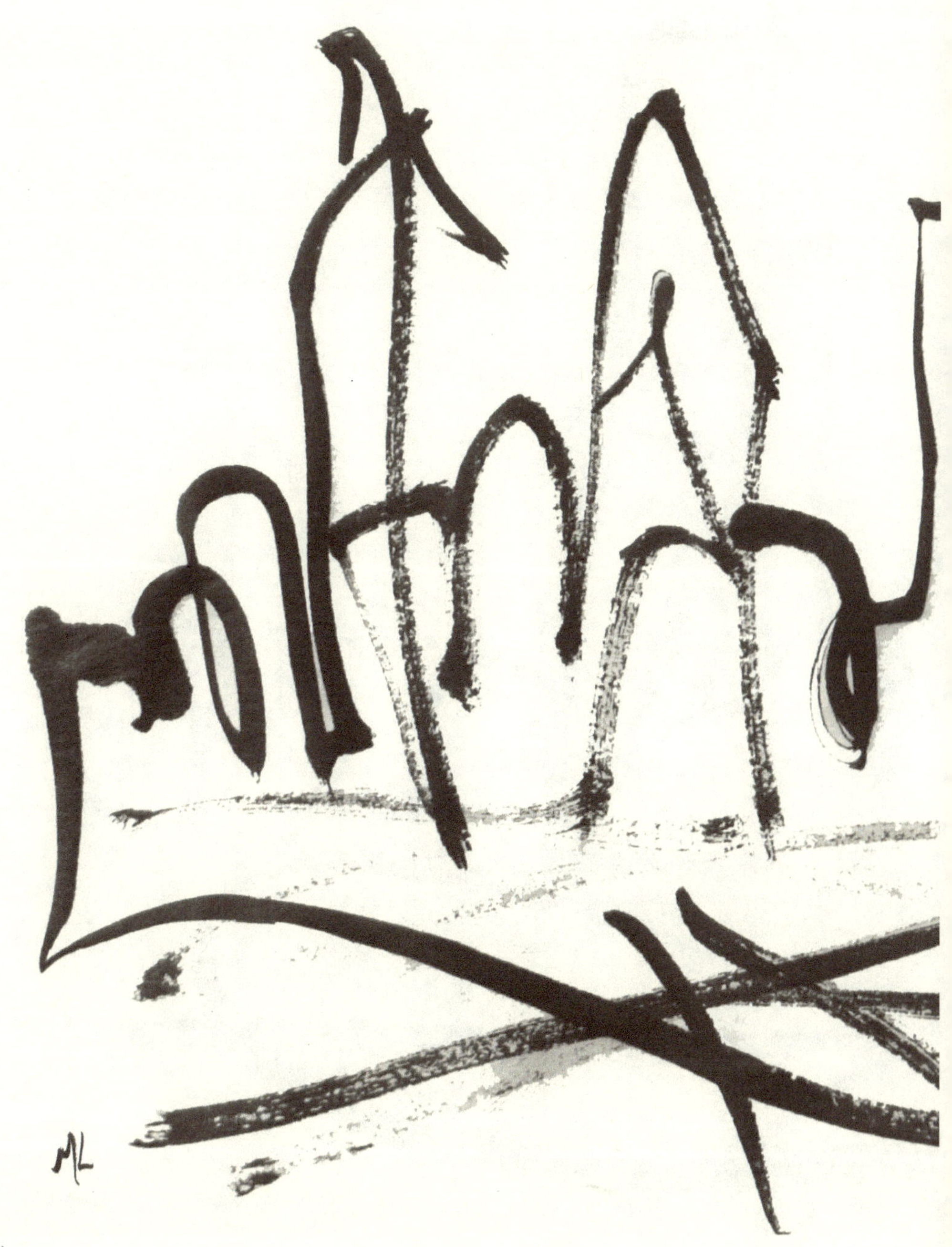

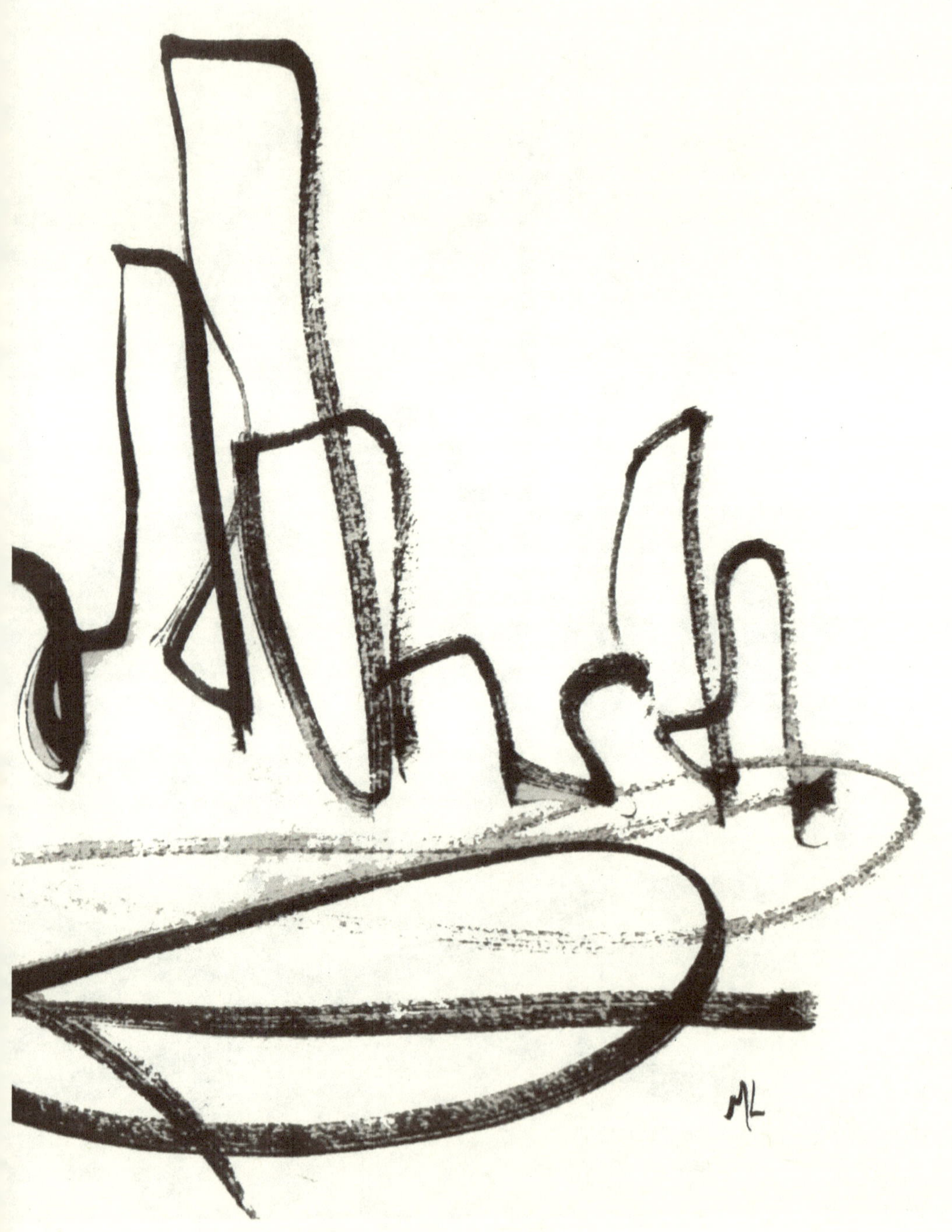

Houston Skyline

Jagged line of my heart

see how it breaks   into so many fractals
calling me back
to a singular life
how it shatters

horses
galloping away
in both worlds   dream & waking

of uneven oak trees
long windy
lunar nights

how the signs keep changing
& how we must read the signs
endless winding highways carry
memories of horses
from one hundred years ago

how to mend a broken heart
broken 3 times
is it possible to really mend what has been broken?

i catch my breath &

go eat *phở* in Midtown

the signs i never understood

being in this state of turmoil

hours & hours traversed

for Indian food

ice skating in the Galleria

sound of blades

swooshing past present & future

it is the body that haunts

desires without discrimination

of verdant moons &

desire indefatigable

[a pyramid driving off a cliff

diving straight into verdant waters]

moments of hunger

moments of silence

fuchsias blossoming

fierce highways byways & bayous incessant flooding

catastrophic rain

to get from here to there

wading through your

scintillating waters

Galveston Time

A sack on a large wooden stick
            sign on wood   a precaution for folks
not to swim further towards the levee

waves roll in & crash incessantly
                                    grey-blue forecasting skies

curious to see a sack so large so perfectly
                                          balanced on the stick

i move closer
            to inspect it

startled   it moves   as if sensing my movements
                              slowly
one edge of the sack
                  then another
                                    begins to lift itself

            how is this possible that an inert object can move itself?
a robot? a new mechanism for spying?

suddenly   a large yellow beak lifts into the air
                                          an eyeball

peaks from the head of the sack

then

wings with an an enormous span

as if at the top of a totem pole

unfolds its massive power

its body voluminous

eyes inspect me intently

vigorously

our eyes meet

it notices that i don't move

my wings at all

not having visible wings

i don't show anything menancing

without further ado

it bends down closes up

tucks away its grandiose pelican self

into a sack presence again

balanced perfectly on a stick

& enters a state between

slumber & vigil

IV

Autumnal Night's Dream

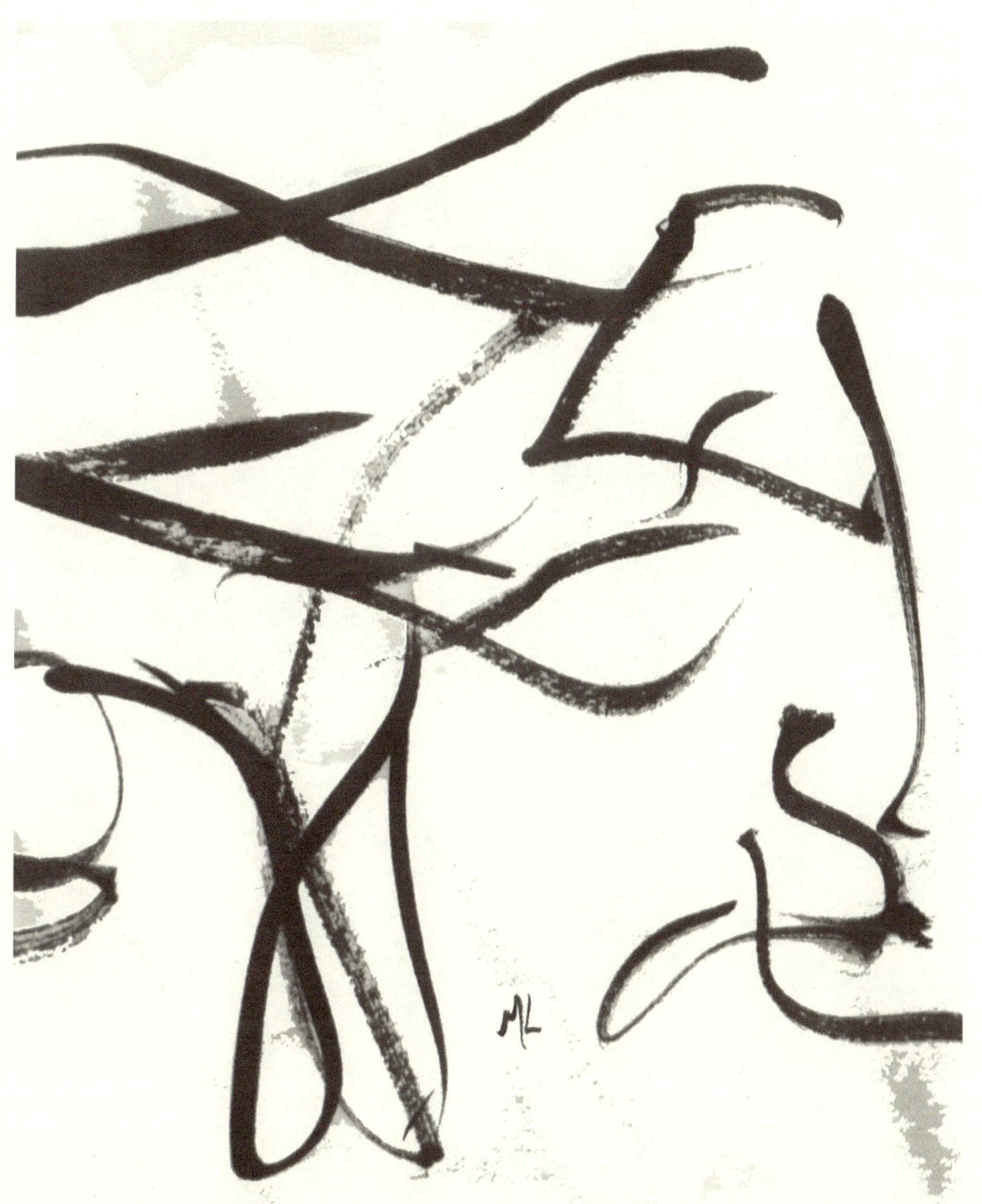

Midwinter in Buenos Aires

the dark-caped man comes on silver wings
swoops down embraces us

arriving at many dimensions at once

paralyzed thought such brilliance —

earth-shattering

such that changes everything
the way i think about dance & the world

that finally makes the world clear
thought fluid movement
that through this compassionate energy

we are saved

then   to speak of the light

moment of concentration   white heat
                                                        an eagle's fierceness flying
                intensity   mental acuity   remembrance
        the body remembers everything

        succumbing to a certain fragrance
                    the opiates of the heart   to stop the bleeding

                ten thousands wings will not do

there are no maps for where we need to go

where we go

no maps   for us my love

all that is life

every cell of my body knows this abundant flowing

everything   real or unreal   those of the flesh or of thought

the night

watches the night watchman

as the guitarist becomes her guitar

the dancer becomes the dance

Particulars

how strange to feel your strength
as soon as i touched you

name the nouns
fingers on wood fingers on strings
the hallowed chord of a guitar

toe on grass nail on toe
the Achilles tendon
at the crossroads of my own knowing

one writes
the particulars
to mean the whole

i've outgrown the red skies
las noches oscuras de Buenos Aires
sin fin
outgrown the need
to be miserable

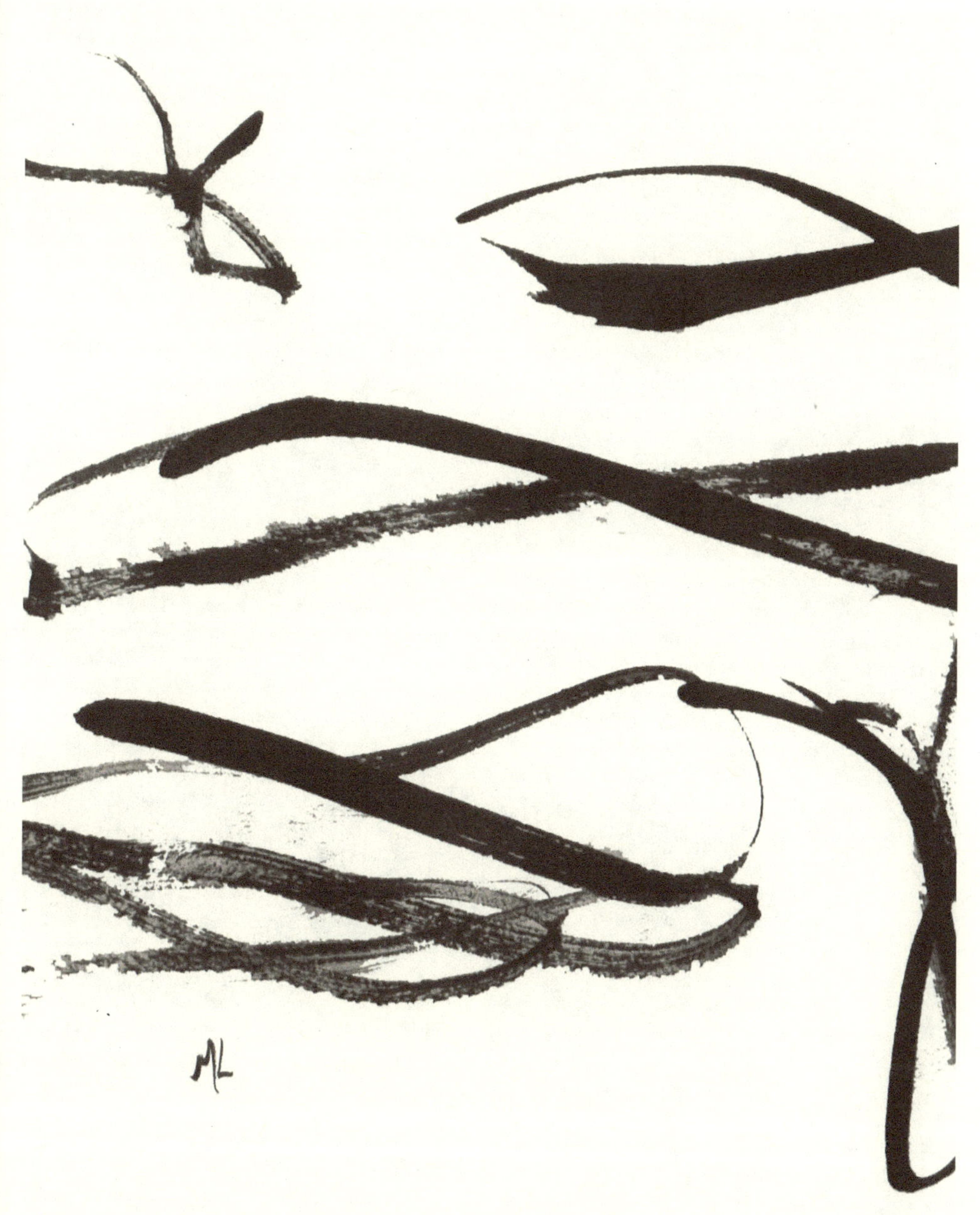
ML

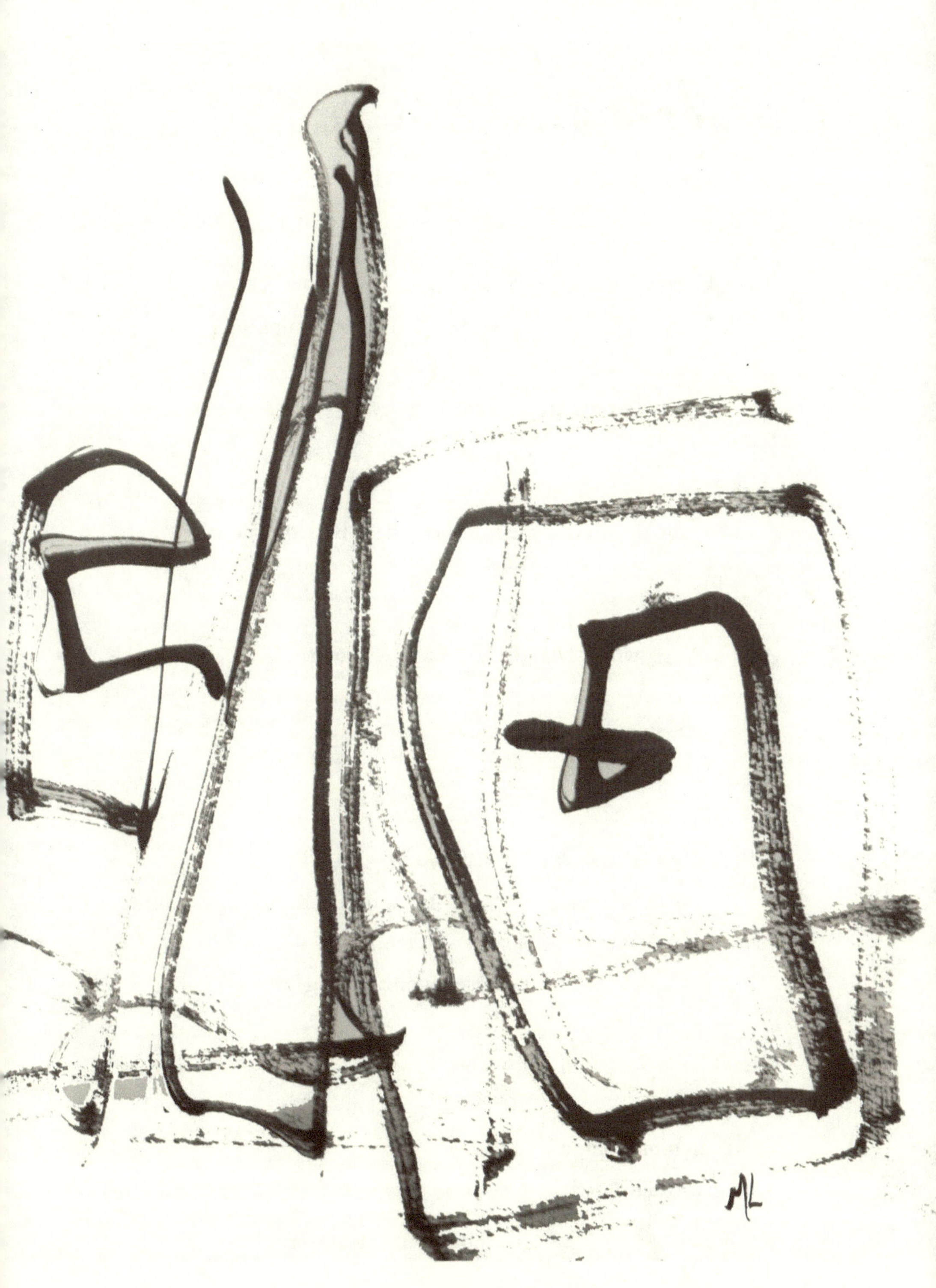

did i ask for exhilaration of the body?

did i ask for lies   constant *mentiras*
did i ask   for *this*   all of *this* complicates

right from the beginning   you were fidgety
        (desde el principio   nervioso)
on the deck   speechless
    on the brim something new   heat heat & hotness

where were you
    when the birds first sang their song?
transmit
    a poetry of sheer beauty

i think in panoramic skies   unstifled
    my algorithm   love multiplied x number of times
a song permeates into the blueness of evening
        cables of unenduring lust

sprinkle dust over my nightly cries
        monks guard my heart
    in monotonous chant
around the blue hotel
        the hotel that never sleeps

Resonance

1

To have much desire   & then none
to love much & then let it all go
the love is there   always

a pigeon's skull beaten on the street
weightless throb   & then it's over
perhaps he will find a young woman who will carry his child
a child with the sonority of a double bass
how can we live our lives remembering our loves?

chime of a miracle unexpected
echo of a tear   undropped still in the eye
resonance of a universe that hears itself
deep tone of a vice   a verse unspoken
unbroken voice of the divine

2

when we go to the river   *Río de la Plata*

we look into its waters   into the vast horizon   pale   murky

full of insinuations

crazy   muffled by desire   stung by music's fire
you talked

at the river   we listen
to the water   oozing melodies
the ear cannot hear
that eyes cannot see

a river full of song
melancholic tangos

i learn to forget your touch   your kisses   everything as if in a stupor

3

skate of a tripping cello bow
to have one's hands consumed by music
to hear music between the heavens   between the stars
visceral stardust

that it existed   exists   & will continue to exist in a sphere
that we cannot see   only feel

the walking wounded
a woman with a thousand bullet holes
the one who loves too much   wrecklessly
the one who puts the first step forward
a fierce nostalgic note —

& i dream of you   what you want
tomorrow i will understand everything

nothing in life   an accident
everything happens for a reason

we must question why

4

my love lost wallowing in the sound of his walrus

double bass

under a fig tree of his own imagination

with no remorse   no courage to continue   no heart to tell the story

hit by the oncoming bus of his own morbidity

swallowing his music

sky drawn with blood

blotched mirror   its beloved

5

cobbled skies of night
of fortune untold   undivinable   blank

fourteen men walk into a room of daisies   trumpets
a line of angry people beating their pots   city of indignant people
hair distraught

four women dream of forever   a kiss that lasts
an orgasm perfect   round   high-pitched

an ultramarine deep   — ocean full of octopi

6

have you seen ink the color of light?
miraculous   everything can be written   seen at once

everything immediately understood
even lies unclaimed
even love denied
mistakes orphaned

the hand   a symptom & proclamation of one's identity
our fingers   appendages that follow our commands

once again the morning rises upon the port city   a Grecian urn
mauve light   rinsing off its night of debauchery
rising into innocence

my gift is perfect   silence azure   pristine

absence so sweet you can taste it

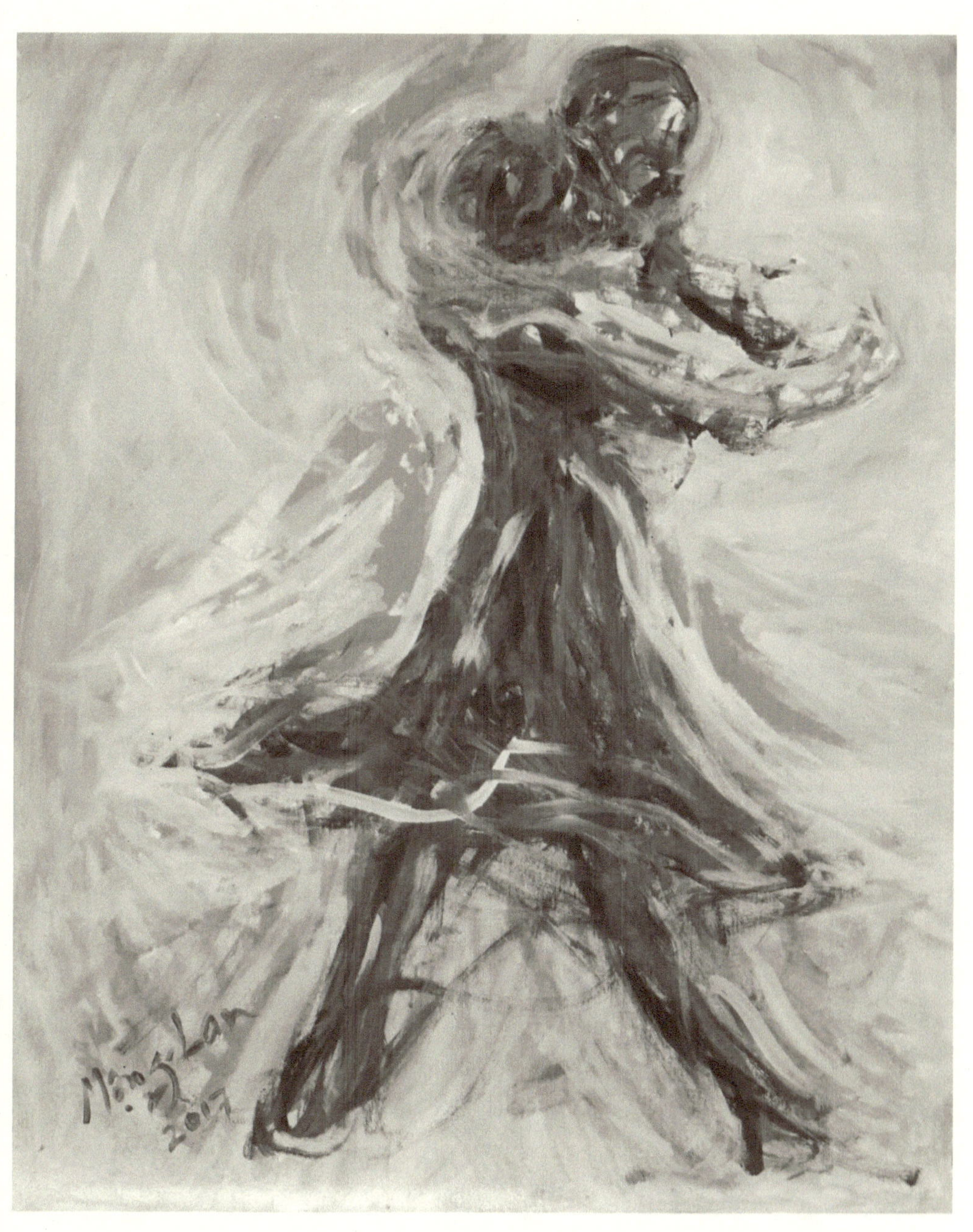

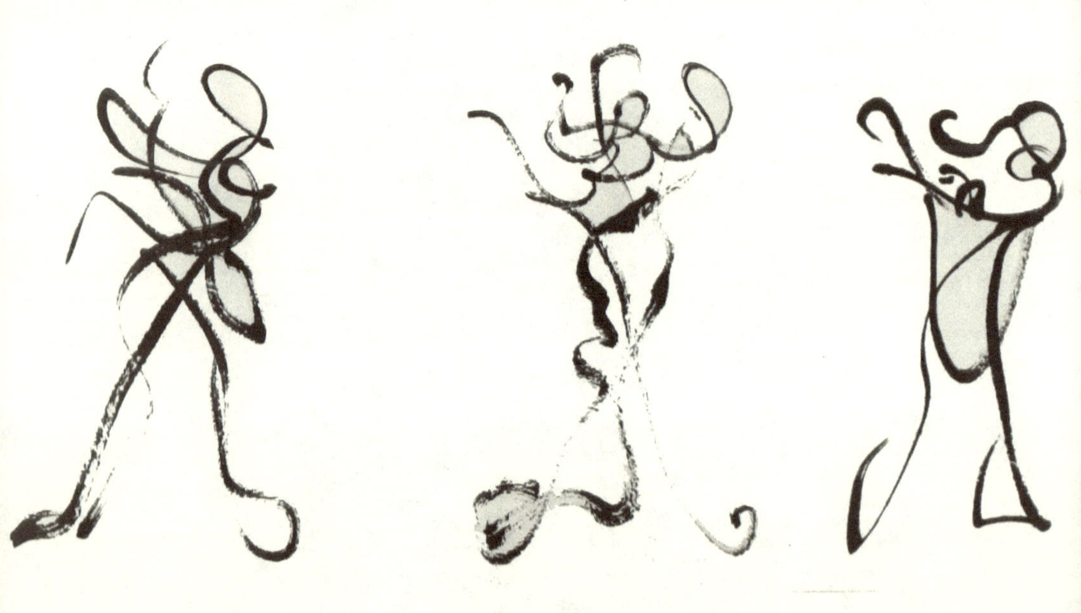

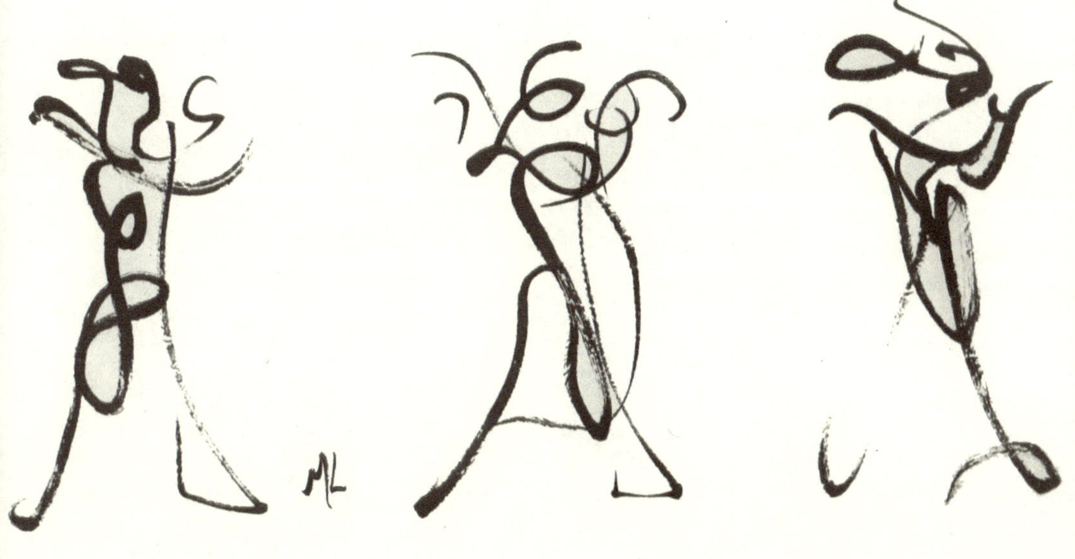
ML

NOTES

All artwork done by Mộng-Lan, different sizes, painted with Japanese ink and brush on rice paper roll, from 11 inches x 11 feet or more, 2017.

Page 5, *paltas*, or avocados, at the time of this publication, now cost three for $40-45 pesos on the streets of Buenos Aires, because of rampant inflation, and only after a period of about five years after orginally writing the poem.

Tango Dancers, page 101, 2.75 ft x 3.4 ft, acrylic on canvas, 2017.

BIOGRAPHY

Mộng-Lan, Vietnamese-American writer, poet, painter, photographer, Argentine tango dancer, singer, multi-instrumental musician, composer, and educator, left her native Việt Nam on the last day of the evacuation of Sài Gòn. Former Stegner Fellow at Stanford University, Fulbright Scholar, she has published seven books of poetry and art, and two chapbooks. Winner of a Pushcart Prize, the Juniper Prize, the Great Lakes Colleges Association's New Writers Awards for Poetry, and other awards, Mộng-Lan's poetry has been nationally and internationally anthologized to include in *Best American Poetry* and *The Pushcart Book of Poetry: Best Poems from 30 Years of the Pushcart Prize.* Mộng-Lan's books include *Song of the Cicadas (Juniper Prize); Why is the Edge Always Windy?; Tango, Tangoing: Poems & Art; Tango, Tangueando: Poemas & Dibujos* (bilingual Spanish-English edition); *Force of the Heart: Tango, Art; One Thousand Minds Brimming: poems & art; Love Poem to Tofu & Other Poems* (poetry & calligraphic art, chapbook). She has also completed a novel, with an excerpt in the *North American Review.*

As a visual artist, Mộng-Lan has exhibited her paintings and photographs for one year in the Capitol House in Washington D.C., in galleries and museums in the United States such as the Dallas Museum of Art, the Museum of Fine Arts in Houston, and in public exhibitions in Tokyo, Seoul, Bali, Bangkok, and Buenos Aires. In conjunction with a grant from the National Endowment for the Arts, she was the Dallas Museum of Fine Arts' inaugural Visual Artist and Poet in Residence in 2005. An exhibition of her paintings and photographs, "The World of Mộng-Lan," ran for six months at the Museum.

As a musician, Mộng-Lan plays the piano and guitar, sings in six languages, and also composes. Her nine albums of jazz piano and tangos also showcase her poetry. She has performed nationally and internationally for cultural organizations and on university campuses.

As a dancer, Mộng-Lan has studied ballet, jazz and flamenco, and for over twenty years has specialized in Argentine tango. A performer & teacher, she has appeared in Buenos Aires, San Francisco, New York City, Tokyo, Bangkok, and elsewhere.

Mộng-Lan's new solo show, *Ocean of Senses: Dream Songs & Tangos* blends original poetry, jazz piano, guitar, dance, story, song, and projections of her artwork.

As an educator, Mộng-Lan has taught at the University of Maryland in Tokyo, University of Arizona, and Stanford University, and has served as a visiting artist-writer at numerous universities, schools, and organizations in the United States and abroad. She took her Master of Fine Arts in creative writing at the University of Arizona. Mộng-Lan has given scores of readings and academic presentations in Argentina, Germany, Indonesia, Japan, Korea, Malaysia, Switzerland, Thailand, and Việt Nam. She travels frequently, both nationally and internationally, to give performances, readings and lectures, teach, show her artwork, and dance tango.

Visit: www.monglan.com

Praise for Mộng-Lan's books

On *Song of the Cicadas* (Juniper Prize Winner)

"In Asian tradition, poetry and visual art go hand in hand, with the collaboration of work, image, and calligraphy. Mộng-Lan's first book renews this tradition for American poetry, and with a startling subject matter. Her poems and drawings dealing with Việt Nam reflect the awe, the anger, and the mourning of the expatriate who returns to the country of her birth .... We sense that she also values what she brings from her own adoptive culture—a new language, a new aesthetic, and the conviction that a woman artist has special insights to offer on the subject of armed conflict and its aftermath. From visual beauty, human suffering, and verbal inventiveness, Mộng-Lan stakes out a poetic territory that is completely her own." —Alford Corn, poet, novelist, critic.

On *Why Is The Edge Always Windy?*

" 'what you've lived through   you are,' says Mộng-Lan in 'Coast,' one of the early poems in this beautiful, spellbinding book, *Why Is The Edge Always Windy?* . . . The lyricism of her writing sings not of the ethereal but of a hard land; her work speaks not of arrested moments but of the tectonic force of history, which, moving at the pace of geological time, presses cultures against each other, folds moments over each other, edges everywhere and always exposed. Indeed, Mộng-Lan's are poems of exposure. Reading them is revelatory."—Lyn Hejinian, poet, translator, UC Berkeley

On *Tango, Tangoing: Poems & Art*

"A mesmerizing accomplishment—four voices at their climax: the dance, if we can call it that, the physics of being, the history and

manual of dark beauty and the *voleos* of line, ink, stanza and voice, layers of loss, desire and the body in ecstatic explosions. Three drops of Lorca, one tincture of María Luisa Bombal and a full *vasija* of Mộng-Lan, a masterpiece, *señores y señoras*. A mathematics of fire."
—Juan Felipe Herrera, U.S. Poet Laureate

On *One Thousand Minds Brimming: poems & art*

"... A true original, unafraid of sentiment and at the height of her artistic prowess, Mộng-Lan's new book proves she remains one of our leading poets."—Ravi Shankar, poet, editor of *Drunken Boat*.

"Mộng-Lan's poems are fresh and real as a street, full of the seriousness of pleasure. She has the same sense of joy that Kenneth Koch loved in the courage to sing, happiness of St.-John Perse. The courage of Frank O'Hara .... The wars and horrors of wars are here, but even disasters and disappearance doesn't stop the poet from celebrating lemons and vegetables I do not know. The Chinese speak of the three perfections: poetry, painting and calligraphy. But Mộng-Lan speaks fo the great imperfections that are better for being so... .. I praise these poems of praise which collapse distance and makes us feel, as O'Hara seemed to say, poetry is just a telephone call away."
—David Shapiro, poet, critic.

www.ingramcontent.com/pod-product-compliance
Lightning Source LLC
LaVergne TN
LVHW091005080826
845145LV00003B/1135

* 9 7 8 0 9 8 2 8 2 2 7 4 6 *